NetWare Answers: Certified Tech Support

**James Nadler and
Don Guarnieri**

Osborne **McGraw-Hill**
Berkeley · New York · St. Louis
San Francisco · Auckland · Bogotá
Hamburg · London · Madrid · Mexico
City · Milan · Montreal · New Delhi
Panama City · Paris · São Paulo
Singapore · Sydney · Tokyo · Toronto

Osborne **McGraw-Hill**
2600 Tenth Street, Berkeley, California 94710, USA

For information on translations or book distributors outside of the U.S.A.,
please write to Osborne McGraw-Hill at the above address.

NetWare Answers: Certified Tech Support

234567890 DOC 9987654

ISBN 0-07-882044-8

Publisher	**Illustrator**
Lawrence Levitsky	Marla Shelasky
Acquisitions Editor	**Series Design**
Scott Rogers	Marla Shelasky
Project Editor	**Quality Control Specialist**
Emily Rader	Joe Scuderi
Computer Designer	**Cover Designer**
Peter F. Hancik	Ted Mader & Assoc.

Contents at a Glance

Contents

Foreword

Few things are as frustrating as having a computer problem that you can't solve. Computer users often spend hours trying to find the answer to a *single* software question! That's why the tech support experts at Corporate Software Incorporated (CSI) have teamed up with Osborne/McGraw-Hill to bring you the **Certified Tech Support Series**—books designed to give you all the solutions you need to fix even the most difficult software glitches.

At Corporate Software, we have a dedicated support staff that handles over 200,000 software questions every month. These experts use the latest hardware and software technology to provide answers to every sort of software problem. CSI takes full advantage of the partnerships that we have forged with all major software publishers. Our staff frequently receives the same training that publishers offer their own support representatives and has access to vendor technical resources that are not generally available to the public.

Thus, this series is based on actual *empirical* data. We've drawn on our support expertise and sorted through our vast database of software solutions to find the most important and frequently asked questions for NetWare. These questions have also been checked and rechecked for technical accuracy and are organized in a way that will let you find the answer you need quickly—providing you with a one-stop tech support solution to your software problems.

No longer do you have to spend hours on the phone waiting for someone to answer your tech support question! You are holding the single, most authoritative collection of answers to your software questions available—the next best thing to having a tech support expert by your side.

We've helped millions of people solve their software problems. Let us help you.

Randy Burkhart
Senior Vice President, Technology
Corporate Software Inc.

Acknowledgments

Osborne/McGraw-Hill would like to thank the following people at Corporate Software, who helped make this book possible: Aaron C., Alex A., Ashish K., Burleigh W., Danny F., Darla C., David B., David F., Doug B., Glenn W., Harry L., James D., Jeanie S., Kathi B., Kevin M., Larry C., Leo S., Linda D., Phil S., Raj P., Wallis O. and William W.

Special thanks to: Mark E., Kim A., Jan R., Bret S., Hank K., Keith M., Loretta B., Mark D., Mickey M. and Scott K.

Introduction

Any software system requires hardware on which it can be run. NetWare, however, requires a local area network, and networks are not just a collection of PCs with some wire strung between them. Even at their simplest, 80X86-based networks are a complex integration of cabling infrastructure, protocols, multiple CPUs, and multiple operating systems. Because a network is designed to deliver shared hardware and software services, these components invariably perform different tasks concurrently. The environment is inevitably multi-vendor, and there is almost never a problem that can adequately be answered by a single manual, because almost everything that goes wrong on a network is a function of the interaction of devices from different publishers and manufacturers. That's exactly why this volume is so important and so useful: it treats NetWare problems in the context of a network environment, and in doing so answers questions from a perspective that simply can't be provided from outside the framework of integration.

If you've purchased this book, the odds are that you are in some position of administrative or supervisory responsibility for your LAN—even if you're an organization of one—or you'd be calling your local support team and getting back to your professional life instead of reading this stuff. It's important to remember that when you're dealing with a LAN, you're dealing with a community of users, and it doesn't take a crashed server to send that community into revolt. More often than not, small problems such as flaky connections, lost files, or garbled print jobs are the most difficult to solve. Just because they're small to you in comparison to network disaster, however, doesn't make them less important to the users who are affected in a particular situation. Try to keep your head and be nice when everyone is breathing down your neck. A clear head makes for strong observational powers, and observation is the key to solving most computer problems. In the long run, your community of users will be happier, calmer, and more helpful in explaining their problems, which will, in turn, facilitate your diagnosis. Also, since you're dealing with an integration environment, try to have some basic tools available—screwdrivers (flat and Philips), hex nut drivers, a cable testing device appropriate to the type of media you're using (Ohmmeter, Brand REX, or Token Ring Cable Tester), a two-position stripper, a flashlight, and a can of compressed air. Fancier and more expensive gear is available, but this list will cover most situations, and it's hard to get anywhere with less.

NetWare Answers: Certified Tech Support is organized into 9 chapters. Each chapter contains questions and answers on a specific area of NetWare, which are categorized in sections by the NetWare version to which they relate. In addition, a list of acronyms is provided, which spells out the acronyms used in this book, as well as many other networking acronyms (Appendix A), and a glossary of definitions which are useful to NetWare users and administrators (Appendix B).

This book also contains the following elements to help you troubleshoot problems and increase your knowledge of NetWare:

Frustration Busters: Special coverage of NetWare topics that have proven confusing to many users. A few minutes spent reading each of these boxes can help you avoid problems from the start.

Tech Tips: Short technical pointers that provide related information or additional insight into a topic addressed in one of the questions.

Tech Terrors: Pitfalls you will want to steer clear of.

Top Ten Tech Terrors

To assemble this book we have tapped the data banks and consultant expertise at Corporate Software, and have identified questions about Novell NetWare called in by people like you, every day. The Top Ten technical issues presented in this chapter are just a few of the many covered in this compendium of answers harvested from the largest technical support company in the United States. So relax—the next time you run into technical difficulty with NetWare, you'll know just where to look for a solution.

Now here they are: ten of the most common problems you're likely to encounter when working with NetWare.

1 What version of IPX and NETX should be used with Windows 3.1?

Windows 3.1 requires NETX 3.26 or higher and IPX 3.10 or higher. For the record, when IPXODI is used, Windows 3.1 requires IPXODI 1.20 or higher. NETX 3.32 or higher is required for DOS 6.*x*, and you must be sure that the SETVER table does not contain an entry for NETX.

Tech Tip: To check for the existence of NETX in SETVER, enter **TYPE SETVER** at the command line. If the NETX entry exists, delete it by entering the statement **SETVER** *D:\pathname* **NETX.COM /DELETE** (where *D:\pathname* is the location of the file) at the command line. You should also check NetWire, Novell's electronic information service on CompuServe, frequently for the latest shell versions. These are usually in a download file called DOSUP*x*, where *x* is the latest number of the file.

2 What does NetWare mean when it displays the message, "A File Server could not be found" after I attempt to run NETX?

This message is generated by the shell when trying to build a connection with the network. A file server did not respond to the connection request and NETX timed out. This could be caused by a loose or malfunctioning cable, a defective network interface card, an incorrect IPX configuration, or a nonfunctioning file server.

At the workstation, check the cable. Is it attached to the workstation? Try unplugging or unscrewing the cable and then reattaching it to the workstation. If the cable goes to a wall mount, see if it is still connected. Is the network card configured properly? Run IPX /I to determine if the configuration matches the board settings. If you are using ODI drivers, be sure that NET.CFG is valid. Is the proper software being loaded? Was the workstation driver changed recently? Examine AUTOEXEC.BAT and make sure all the necessary drivers have been loaded. If necessary, reboot the workstation and watch as each driver loads. If an error occurs on one of the drivers, it will be reported, but the boot process probably will not stop.

Check to see that the file server is running and is not locked up. Are other persons logged in? Is the server attached to the cable? Is AUTOEXEC.NCF correct? If you can get to the server console, type **CONFIG** to see what configuration is loaded. To see if the server is communicating with the network, enter **TRACK ON**.

Is it possible that there are other cabling problems? Check the network cabling. Is the cable attached to the hub? Was anyone working on the cabling system, or was other construction work done near your workstation? Try to find the cable that goes to your workstation, and see if it is still plugged into the concentrator. If you are on a bus network, other workstations on the same segment should also be having problems. Check to see if the terminators are intact.

Since upgrading to VLMs, I receive the following error message whenever I print: "Windows Cannot Write to this File. Disk May be Full." I increased the parameter for FILEHANDLES in NET.CFG, but the problem persists. Why?

This problem often occurs when NETX is used as the shell, instead of the VLMs. If you installed Windows support for the VLMs, you must use them rather than NETX. With VLMs, the FILEHANDLES statement in NET.CFG is no longer valid. To solve the problem, increase the FILES statement to about 100 in CONFIG.SYS.

After running the installation program for the NetWare DOS Requester, I get this error message when loading Windows: "The NetWare VLM is not loaded or is not configured correctly." What does this mean?

Like the previous question, this most often occurs when NETX is used as the shell, instead of the VLMs. If you installed Windows support with the VLMs, you must use them rather than NETX.

5 The following message appears when I attempt to log in to a NetWare 4.x file server: "Your current context is xxxxx.xxxxx. The user specified does not exist in this context. LOGIN will try to find the user in the server context." Why?

Tech Tip: In the commands specified to the right, CN is the Common Name (user name), O is the Organization, and OU is the Organization Unit. The periods are qualifiers. The naming tree is hierarchical, so you can have multiple organizational units.

This message is displayed when LOGIN cannot find your user name in the current context or bindery context. To resolve the problem, specify the full name of the user when logging in, in this format:

LOGIN *servername* /CN=*xxxx*.O=*xxxx*

You can also specify the default context in the NET.CFG file. To do so, add the following line to the NetWare DOS Requester section of NET.CFG:

NAME CONTEXT="OU=*xxxx*.OU=*xxxx*.O=*xxxx*"

There is also a command called CX that displays the current context. Using CX in conjunction with other parameters allows you to change the current context.

6 How can I edit the system login script on a NetWare 4.x server?

NetWare 4.x does not have a system login script. The closest equivalent is the *container login script*; however, it only applies to users in that container. The system login script remains on the server (in SYS:SYSTEM) after an upgrade, and may still be accessed by users of bindery emulation. In addition to the container login script, NetWare 4.x uses a *profile login script* and a *user login script*.

Tech Tip: A good way to remember the order in which the NetWare 4.x scripts execute is by thinking of the acronym, CPU—C stands for container, P for profile, and U for user.

7 Do printers use a NetWare user connection?

It depends on how you set up your print server(s). Loading PSERVER.EXE on a dedicated workstation occupies a user connection, whereas loading PSERVER.NLM at the server console does not. In addition, a printer set up using RPRINTER.EXE on a non-dedicated workstation does not use a connection.

8 Why do I receive memory errors when executing CAPTURE in a login script on a NetWare 4.x server?

The versions of LOGIN.EXE and CAPTURE.EXE that ship with NetWare 4.x require more memory than in previous versions of NetWare. Executing the CAPTURE command in a login script causes LOGIN and CAPTURE to load simultaneously, consuming all of the workstation's available memory. To resolve this issue, exit from the login script to a batch file that runs CAPTURE, or run CAPTURE from the command line after logging into the network.

This problem may also indicate you have too many TSRs loaded prior to login. Remember, the NetWare shell takes up memory on the workstation. Try loading some of the TSRs *after* logging in to the network, or if you have DOS 5 or higher, use the LOADHIGH statement.

9 Can I use SYSCON to administer my NetWare 4.x server?

In a NetWare 4.x environment, SYSCON can only be used to administer bindery emulation users. The replacements for SYSCON in NetWare 4.x are NETADMIN (for DOS), and NWADMIN (for Windows); these must be used to administer NDS users. (NDS contains descriptions of all the objects on the network, not just the server.)

10 What version of the NetWare Requester do I need to work with IBM OS/2 2.1?

The NetWare Requester (also known as The NetWare Workstation for OS/2) version 2.01 provides the most reliable connection between a NetWare file server and IBM OS/2 2.1. Check NetWire often; the Requester is always in development.

Network
Administration

Depending on whom you're talking to, NetWare gets described in different ways. Some call it an operating system, others call it merely a protocol. Networks are more than operating systems and protocols, however, and all network operating systems must address physical considerations.

NetWare runs on just about every kind of cabling plant in popular use today—coax, twisted pair, and fiber—in just about every flavor of network topology you can think of—ARCnet, Ethernet, Token Ring, AppleTalk, VMS, and so on. In addition, there are NetWare drivers for virtually every piece of hardware that might find its way into a modern network installation. Though the integration of all these aspects makes networking a powerful and interesting discipline, it also makes the job of troubleshooting a network particularly challenging. Because there is a natural interplay between components from so many different manufacturers, one source rarely contains the answer to more than the simplest question. In some areas—printing or file services, for instance—this elusiveness is less poignantly felt, simply because the scope of factors is narrow and more restricted to NetWare. With others, in particular network administration, which pertains to everything from the cabling plant to issues that defy categorization, you must learn to think inductively about how the network operates. Knowing NetWare solutions helps, but don't depend on your knowledge of NetWare alone to solve every problem.

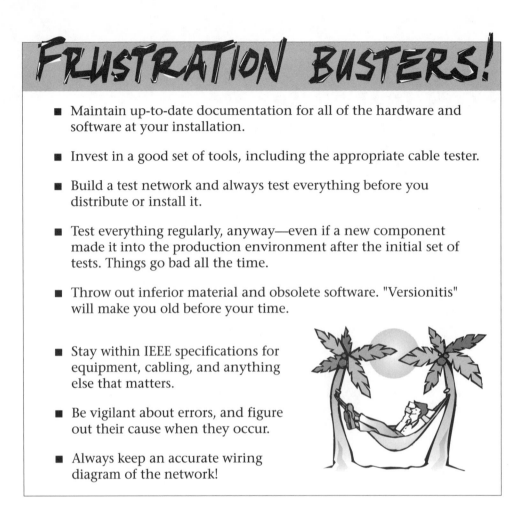

FRUSTRATION BUSTERS!

- Maintain up-to-date documentation for all of the hardware and software at your installation.

- Invest in a good set of tools, including the appropriate cable tester.

- Build a test network and always test everything before you distribute or install it.

- Test everything regularly, anyway—even if a new component made it into the production environment after the initial set of tests. Things go bad all the time.

- Throw out inferior material and obsolete software. "Versionitis" will make you old before your time.

- Stay within IEEE specifications for equipment, cabling, and anything else that matters.

- Be vigilant about errors, and figure out their cause when they occur.

- Always keep an accurate wiring diagram of the network!

What is the difference between a file server and an application server?

File server is a generic term for a device or process that manages commonly used programs and data on a LAN. These items usually include print services, communications services, word processing programs and files, electronic mail, and so on. Furthermore, a user normally establishes an explicit connection to a file server through a drive mapping.

Application servers act as client machines on a LAN and require the presence of a file server to provide low-level transport protocols. An application server usually provides a specific service on a LAN at the discrete request of an application (the client). For example, a database server might retrieve certain records for display in an accounting application; a compute server might perform certain number-crunching routines at the request of a modeling application. The calling application—rather than the user—establishes the dialog with the server. The service is transparent to the user, and the connection is typically made through a request using a protocol such as TCP/IP, Named Pipes, or NetBIOS, though certain NLM database applications use IPX/SPX.

What is the difference between network drives and search drives?

Network drives are logical drive letters. They are pointers to physical drive volumes and are attached using the NetWare MAP command. For example,

```
MAP F:=SERVER1\SYS:PROGRAMS/WINDOWS
```

makes F: the drive for the Windows directory on SERVER1. Programs that exist in the WINDOWS directory, however, will be found by calling applications only when F: is explicitly referenced. For example, a program calling NOTEPAD.EXE must refer to F: NOTEPAD.EXE in order to succeed.

Search drives, on the other hand, are added to the beginning of the DOS Path. Physical drive volumes can be mapped to up to 16 search drives (S1 through S16) without diminishing the number of available network drives. These drives are searched, in succession beginning with S1, by any calling program, for an executable file that might exist in them. For example,

```
MAP INSERT S1:=SERVER1\SYS:DOS
```

would effectively place all DOS commands in the path, and cause the DOS directory to be the first directory searched after the path named in AUTOEXEC.BAT. DOS commands such as TYPE that normally do not execute on files in the path will succeed if the file is located in the NetWare search path.

Is there an easy and reliable way to check the cabling before starting the file server?

There's easy, and then there's reliable. For the greatest reliability, you'll want to invest in a cable tester. Use an RJ cable tester for UTP, or an OHM meter for coax. The RJ device consists of two small boxes, each with RJ jacks. If the cable is connected correctly, the LEDs light up green. If the cable is connected but the pairs are reversed, the LEDs light up red. If the cables are *not* connected correctly, some or all of the LEDs will fail. With an OHM meter, you need to check the resistance on the cable. If the cable is intact, both terminators are attached, and none of the computers on the network are attached or powered up, a Coaxial Ethernet network should have a reading of 25 ohms.

If you don't have the cable testing equipment on hand, here's a simpler but less informative test. Boot each workstation on the net from DOS, load IPX.COM (without NETX), and run COMCHECK. COMCHECK will prompt you for a unique name with which to identify each workstation, and will test for responses from other nodes on the net at regular intervals (15 seconds by default). If there is no response from a node within 60 seconds, each connected workstation will display a message with the name of the workstation(s) that is failing. You will find the COMCHECK program on one of the following disks, depending on which version of NetWare you have:

- NetWare 286: Diagnostic disk
- NetWare 386 3.0: SHGEN-1 disk
- NetWare 386 3.*x*: DOS/DOS ODI Workstation Services disk

Can we use our existing telephone wiring to add workstations to our 10BaseT network?

This is often possible, but keep in mind the following caveats:

- It is recommended that the UTP wiring be grade level 3 or higher. If the wiring is more than ten years old, or the phone system is from the Centronics days, you probably do not have level 3.

- The cable must have two twisted pairs available for each workstation.
- Be sure not to exceed the maximum single segment length of 328 feet or 100 meters.

What does an uninterruptible power supply do?

An *uninterruptible power supply (UPS)* is meant to regulate standard power, as well as keep the network going for a short period of time after a power failure by providing temporary power to the server for an orderly shutdown. A true UPS uses AC voltage (from the wall) to charge the battery, and then uses the battery to feed power back to the computer, as shown in Figure 2-1. This protects the computer from temporary power outages, and many times the UPS has a filter to prevent power spikes.

A *standby power supply (SPS)* is similar to a UPS and may be in more common use. In an SPS, the battery does not provide continuous power to the computer, but rather waits for the power to fail before switching to battery. UPS/SPS systems will

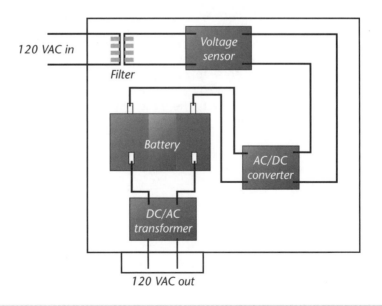

FIGURE 2-1   An uninterruptible power supply

usually notify users that AC power to the server has been lost. The UPS usually is connected to the LAN via the mouse port on a server. Older systems use a connector on the disk coprocessor board (DCB).

Tech Tip: The Micro Channel version of the DCB does not support UPS monitoring; however all Micro Channel machines do have a mouse port.

What's the difference between a physical drive and a logical drive?

Physical drives are actual disks (hard or floppy) that you could feel and touch. *Volume names* are logical groupings of physical disk space. Volume names can consist of up to 11 characters, and a volume can span multiple physical drives. For a workstation to use a drive on a NetWare server, you must assign the drive an identifier to which the workstation's local operating system—typically DOS or OS/2—can refer; this identifier is always a letter, followed by a colon.

Logical drives are a convenient way of providing an alias for some or all of a disk volume. Normally the logical drive designations A: and B: are reserved for local floppy drives on a workstation. If there are local hard drives, they are labeled sequentially beginning with C:. Letter designations for network drives can begin with the next letter after the last one used on the workstation, but normally they start with F: by convention.

NetWare allows you to assign logical drive letters to each directory on a volume using the MAP command. These assignments are valid only for that computing session, and are usually invoked by a login script. For example, consider a server called SERVER1 where the primary volume (SYS) contains these directories:

```
┌── PROGRAMS
│   ├─ 1 2 3
│   └─ WORDPERFECT
├── USERS
├── DOS
└── MAIL
```

The following statement will make G: appear to the local workstation as a complete drive containing all of the directories from SYS, beginning in the subdirectory PROGRAMS:

```
MAP G:=SERVER1/SYS:PROGRAMS
```

What does NetWare mean by the message, "*server name* connection termination in 1 minute"?

This is a message from the network administrator, indicating that the workstation on which the message appears is going to lose its connection to the network very shortly (in 60 seconds). When you see this message, save all important work, close all files and applications, and log off immediately! If you don't know for certain to the contrary, the odds are that your work is stored on the server, and it will be difficult to continue working normally once the connection is broken. This message can be the result of anything from server maintenance to a bomb scare.

Tech Tip: Make a copy on a local floppy drive of that important spreadsheet or document with which you're working. If the network goes down for a while, you might be able to continue working elsewhere if your data is available and portable.

What does NetWare mean by the message, "You have no rights to copy to the specified directory"?

Each user has a set of rights on the network called trustee assignments, which determine the various privileges governing your right to work with programs and data on the network. Rights can be granted to an individual user or a group of users, and pertain to specific directories on the network. The following table defines all of the possible rights for a NetWare directory:

Abbreviation	Name	Allowed Actitivities
F	Filescan	View directory entries
R	Read	Read files
W	Write	Save files
M	Modify	Change files
E	Erase	Delete files

Abbreviation	Name	Allowed Actitivities
C	Create	Create directories and files
A	Access Control	Grant rights to others
S	Supervisor	All rights

In order to copy a directory, you must have Read and Filescan rights in the source directory, and Create rights in the target directory. To see the rights granted to you, look at the trustee directory assignments in your user profile, or type the command **RIGHTS** in the directory in question.

What does NetWare mean by the message, "Directory is not locatable"?

It means NetWare can't figure out which directory you're looking for. This usually occurs because you've misspelled the directory or part of its path. For example,

```
MAP G:\PROGRAMS\DB\PARADOX\MYPROG
```

won't work if MYPROG is really on the path \PROGRAMS \DATABASE\PARADOX\MYPROG. Or you may have mapped the directory to a drive other than the one specified in your command. For example,

```
CD G:\PROGRAMS\DATABASE\PARADOX\MYPROG
```

won't work if \PROGRAMS\DATABASE\PARADOX\MYPROG is mapped to F:. A NetWare failure to locate the directory you are looking for can occur in a MAP or INCLUDE statement in your login script or from the command prompt.

How can I change a password?

When you run SETPASS, NetWare prompts you for the existing password, and then allows you to enter a new one. If you are a supervisor or equivalent, you can press ENTER at the prompt for the old password, the utility will continue, and you can create a new password even if you don't know the old one.

Tech Terror: When you create a user in NetWare, the name can be as long as 47 characters, but DOS will only recognize 8 characters in names of files and directories. This can cause some problems. For example, SUPERVISOR is 10 characters long, but DOS would truncate it to SUPERVIS. This could lead to unusual results when the variable *%login_name* in the system login script tries to place the user in his or her home directory.

How do I change the attributes for a file?

When a file is created on a Novell NetWare volume, the default attributes are nonshareable read/write. After you create the file, you can change its attributes by executing a FLAG command from the system prompt. Use the following syntax:

FLAG *filename.txt /+switch -switch +switch...*

The switches for FLAG are listed in the following table:

Switch	Name	Description
A	Archive Needed	Equal to the DOS archive bit. Used by backup utilities to know if a file has been modified.
X	Execute Only	Can be assigned only by a supervisor to a COM or EXE file and *cannot be removed.* Prevents users from copying the files.
RO	Read Only	This switch also assigns Delete Inhibit and Rename Inhibit flags. Users must have Modify rights to change this attribute.

Switch	Name	Description
S	Shareable	Allows more than one user to use the file at the same time.
H	Hidden	Hides a file from the DOS DIR command, but the file will appear in NetWare's NDIR if the user has Filescan rights.
SY	System	Hides a file from the DOS DIR command and prevents a user from deleting or copying the file.
T	Transactional	Protects the file with transaction tracking system (TTS), which ensures that modified files have all changes completed successfully or no changes are made. Important for database files.
P	Purge	Assigned to a directory to purge any deleted file immediately. The SALVAGE utility cannot recover files once they are purged.
RA	Read	Enables the file for read.
WA	Write Audit	Enables the file for write.
CI	Copy Inhibit	This switch is for Macintosh files only.
DI	Delete Inhibit	Prevents users from deleting a file or directory even if they have rights to erase. Users with Modify rights can remove this attribute and delete the file.
RI	Rename Inhibit	Same as Delete Inhibit, except applies to renaming the file or directory.
ALL	All	Adds all flags to the file.

Switch	Name	Description
N	Normal	Clears all flags and assigns Read/Write flag.
SUB	Subdirectory	Allows the attributes to be applied to directories or subdirectories.

Tech Terror: The FLAG.EXE file that originally shipped with NetWare 386 will return a DOS error code even when the program executes correctly. This becomes a problem if you are using a batch file that includes the statement IF ERRORLEVEL 1 THEN GOTO. DOS normally returns an error code of 1 if the program did not execute correctly, but the Novell 386 FLAG.EXE returns a 1 whether it fails or not.

What is the difference between the directory space restriction and the user restriction?

Both of these settings are supervisor controls. The user restriction determines the total amount of disk space that can be accessed by an individual user, and is set through either SYSCON or DSPACE. The directory space restriction, introduced with NetWare 386, caps the maximum space available in a specific (restricted) directory but sets no limit for any individual user. This restriction is set using the NetWare DSPACE utility.

Tech Terror: Once a directory space restriction limit is met, empty space on the volume is unavailable even if it is free. So if you're running out of room for that 2GB spreadsheet containing the next ten years' precious financial projections, you'd better get the administrator on the phone right now.

What is the difference between an internal router and an external router?

An *internal router* exists within a file server. An *external router* exists in a device external to the server—in other words, a workstation other than the file server (usually a dedicated PC), or a dedicated routing device. In either case, internal or external, the router is created by placing more than one network card in the device (you may have up to four).

For the internal router, configure each card with unique settings, load the LAN drivers, and the file server does the routing automatically. The external PC router requires the presence of a memory-resident program (TSR) called ROUTER.EXE. To generate ROUTER.EXE, run ROUTEGEN. This configures the external router for the type of network interface card: IRQ, I/O port, and so on. ROUTER.EXE can be run from the AUTOEXEC.BAT file and loaded automatically at startup. Dedicated external routers may contain a firmware equivalent to the ROUTER program.

Can interrupts cause problems accessing a server across a Novell router?

Yes. Each card in a router must have a unique interrupt setting; conflicting interrupts will cause problems. Also some interrupt settings may not be appropriate. For example, some cards may be set to Interrupt 2, and others to Interrupt 9 (these are the same). These are the interrupts used in an IBM AT-compatible personal computer and should be avoided. In addition, verify that you have the latest drivers from the relevant network card manufacturers.

What is the NET$ERR.LOG file?

NetWare logs all error messages in this file. This is convenient because you may not always be around when one of these messages echoes to the server console. If something serious happens on the net, odds are that you will know about it before you see headlines about it at the server console. The NET$ERR.LOG file may have some historical interest for you, but it is of little use as an interactive diagnostic tool. Monitor the size of this file, and when it grows so large that it's wasting needed disk space, print out a hard copy for your records. Then either clear the error log (through SYSCON) or delete the file entirely, and NetWare will create a new file if and when errors occur.

What is NetWire?

NetWire is Novell's electronic information service on CompuServe. It is a valuable service, available 24 hours a day, that contains several different forums where you can ask questions of experts. You can download a variety of technical information, including the latest product patches. For CompuServe information, call 800-524-3383.

What files do I need to run NetWare for SAA with NetWare 4.0?

You need the following files, which you can download from the NOVLIB section of NetWire:

PTF400.EXE
PTF401.EXE
PTF402.EXE
PTF403.EXE
PTF404.EXE
PTF40X.EXE

Downloading all six files takes approximately 5 hours if you use a 2400-baud modem, or 1¼ hours if you use a 9600-baud modem.

Broadcast messages halt my application servers (WordPerfect Office, Lotus Notes, SQL, and others) with a message on the 25th line of the display, until someone manually clears the message by pressing CTRL-ENTER. What can I do to avoid this interruption of service?

In order to avoid this message:

```
>> PLEASE LOGOUT IN 5 MINUTES !!!                    (CTRL-ENTER to clear)
```

add the command CASTOFF ALL to the application server's login script or batch file. This should eliminate all but the most serious messages. CASTOFF ALL must be loaded after login. In NetWare 4.0, the equivalent is SEND /A=N.

Tech Tip: If you are using a backup program that saves to removable media such as an optical disk, all users receive an error message when the volume is full. This message is a broadcast message and overrides

CASTOFF and the SET VOL LOW WARN ALL USERS=OFF statement in the AUTOEXEC.NCF. The only way around this is to use the command CASTOFF ALL, which eliminates all messages from any source.

What does NetWare mean by the message, "*server name* Connection time expired. Please log out"?

You're about to be disconnected from the network. User accounts can be governed by a time limit, as established by the administrator in SYSCON. About five minutes will pass between the first appearance of this message and the server's disconnection of the session. Save all files and log out.

My network is slowing down—everyone is experiencing poor performance. How can I begin to diagnose this problem?

The most common causes for poor network performance are not related to NetWare. First, look at how many users are on the network. If you've been adding new users, you may have a traffic issue. Increased traffic can dramatically affect network performance. Even if the population has remained the same, your existing users may be doing things to occupy the server all the time. Are continuous file copies occurring? Are uncharacteristically large files appearing from new application sources such as imaging programs? Are you backing up the server during work hours? If you're using Ethernet, have you extended the network using too many repeaters? Have you installed new network interface cards in the server? This list is endless. All of these things (and combinations of them) can *and do* affect performance. Diagnosing them is beyond the scope of this book, but we can offer general advice: Look at what has changed on the network. Something always has, and therein lies the first clue to solving your problem.

One way in which NetWare can cause performance degradation is through inadequate available cache blocks. Cache blocks indicate low server memory. Check the MONITOR program to determine the Available Cache Blocks number. As a rule of thumb, Available Cache Blocks should be approximately 30% of Total Available Cache Blocks. If the number falls below this threshold, consider adding more memory to your server, or reducing consumption by unloading unused NLM modules. If you find that the number for Available Cache Blocks has fallen significantly below 1,000, consider immediate action to increase the total to avoid a system failure.

Also consider setting the "Set turbo FAT re-use wait time" parameter to 30 minutes. This allows the server to keep its FAT in memory longer, waiting out the slowdown of the network and eliminating the need to run VREPAIR. However, you may want to examine the setup of your network first to see what else may be causing the slowdown.

Tech Tip: You may experience slow performance or intermittent connections on an IBM Token Ring LAN using twisted pair cable (Type 3). IBM's specification for twisted pair cable requires six twists per foot. It's possible your cable is called IBM Type 3 but doesn't adhere to this standard. Performance problems have been documented for cable with only two twists per foot and an even number of workstations on the LAN.

What are Application Loadable Modules?

Application Loadable Modules (ALMs) are used with AppWare, a Novell software layer designed to simplify the development of network applications. ALMs are pre-existing and interchangeable software modules that developers can use to build new applications. ALMs can be simple or complex. Eventually, ALMs associated with graphical user interfaces, database management, multimedia, serial communications, document imaging, and storage all will be available.

The AppWare bus and ALMs are similar to a PC system board and interchangeable printed circuit boards. ALMs related to such tasks as file system management, printing, messaging, and database management can be plugged into the AppWare bus just as boards are plugged into a system board. When ALMs are plugged into the AppWare bus, their functionality becomes rapidly accessible for building new applications.

How can I create a workstation boot diskette?

The exact content of a boot diskette will vary depending on an enormous number of factors, such as the type of hardware you are running, versions of drivers and software, the way in which you want your workstation configured, and so on. However, certain elements are basic. You must use a formatted, bootable floppy diskette containing the IPX.COM and NETX.COM. Include a CONFIG.SYS file with at least these parameters:

```
FILES=number
BUFFERS=number
SHELL=COMMAND.COM /E:512/P
```

and an AUTOEXEC.BAT file containing at least these statements:

```
IPX
NETX
F: (where F is a valid network drive that stores LOGIN.EXE)
LOGIN
```

If you're using ODI drivers, your AUTOEXEC.BAT would contain these statements:

```
LSL
XXXXX.COM (NIC card ODI driver)
IPXODI
VLM or NETX
```

Can I undelete a file I deleted from a network drive?

You can use the menu-driven NetWare utility called SALVAGE.EXE to recover deleted files that have not been purged. SALVAGE will not recover purged files, or files that were marked with the purge attribute when they were deleted. To recover a deleted file, type **SALVAGE** at the command line. Select View/Recover Deleted Files from the Salvage menu, as shown here:

```
┌─────────────────────────────────────┐
│           Main Menu Options          │
├─────────────────────────────────────┤
│ Salvage From Deleted Directories     │
│ Select Current Directory             │
│ Set Salvage Options                  │
│ View/Recover Deleted Files           │
└─────────────────────────────────────┘
```

You must have Create rights for the file you are trying to salvage in order for the salvage operation to succeed.

Tech Tip: When a directory has been deleted in addition to its files, SALVAGE places the deleted files in a directory called DELETED.SAV.

Can I force users to log out at night?

Yes. With SYSCON, set a time restriction for users. This will automatically log those users out at a given time.

Tech Terror: This is dangerous stuff. When NetWare kicks users off the network, it does not do any housekeeping for them, such as saving open files, closing applications, and so on. In addition, users in the middle of a session will have to reboot. Be sure to post advance notice of these restrictions in places where people are likely to see them (e-mail, for instance), and if possible, broadcast a warning several times before actually forcing users out. There are also several third-party utilities that can do this, as well as save the files before logging out the station.

Windows users get a black screen with a blinking cursor in the upper-left corner when entering a DOS dialog box or DOS application, and then the system hangs. What's wrong?

This problem is known as The Black Screen of Death. It can be caused by memory conflicts or incompatible IPXODI, LSL, or VIPX drivers under Windows or Windows for Workgroups. The solution is to download the file BSDUP1.EXE from NetWire. This file contains information on the problem, new versions of these driver files, and text on how to use them.

I'm trying to connect Windows for Workgroups 3.1 to a Novell NetWare 3.x network, and I'm using ARCnet interface cards on my workstations. In the Novell NetWare option in the Networks section of the Windows Control Panel, I see the error message, "The network Novell NetWare cannot be added because Windows for Workgroups does not support this network with your ARCnet adapter." What does it mean?

Windows for Workgroups does not currently support ARCnet interface cards for Novell NetWare. Windows for Workgroups does support the Microsoft network transport protocol (NetBEUI) and the Novell network transport protocol (IPX) by way of ODI or NDIS drivers on the same network adapter card, by including the Novell-compatible protocol, MSIPX. MSIPX supports Token Ring and Ethernet Media Access Control (MAC) header formats, but not token-passing bus network header formats such as ARCnet.

Tech Tip: ARCnet's data packets are smaller than NetWare's, so IPX fragments the ARCnet packets for transmission, and then reconstructs them at the other end. However, when you use an ARCnet NIC with Windows for Workgroups, the ARCnet NDIS driver emulates Ethernet protocol and uses Ethernet header formats, so that Windows for Workgroups recognizes data packets sent along the ARCnet network. The problem occurs because NetWare is expecting fragmented ARCnet data packets and does not recognize data in an Ethernet header format.

How do I run Windows for Workgroups with ODI and NETX in NetWare 4.0?

Use the ODINSUP.COM file found in DOSUP7.ZIP. Check the ODINSUP.DOC file for any special information, and then follow these steps:

1. Install Windows for Workgroups normally.
2. Alter the Setup to use Novell ODI drivers and the ODINSUP.COM file.
3. Load the current VLMs.

What does NetWare mean by the messages, "Token ring status beaconing. Status = 520 (or 420)" and "Alert condition has been corrected"?

They indicate a failed component in a token ring network. When a workstation has not received the token from its upstream neighbor on the ring, that workstation sends a beacon packet to the active monitor on the ring. The active monitor then disconnects the workstation that is not responding and returns the second message. To fix the problem, isolate the point of failure in the token ring card, adapter cable, cable connector, or MAU port.

What does NetWare mean by the messages, "Targeted EXITS are not supported on this machine type" and "The EXIT command followed by a string is not supported on this machine"?

The first of these messages will occur when EXIT is called by a program name; the other occurs when EXIT is called from a batch file. If you change the long machine type in SHELL.CFG to anything other than IBM_PC, you receive the error when exiting in a login script. This can be solved by adding the command PCCOMPATIBLE to the login script. This tells NetWare to allow the EXIT command on IBM-compatible equipment.

When I restore the bindery, trustee assignments are lost. What happened to them?

Trustee assignments are linked to the bindery information but are physically stored with the directory entry—*not in the bindery files*. So if you use BINDFIX to back up the binderies, bring them to another server, and then do a BINDREST, the trustee assignments are lost. To maintain the assignments when you back up the bindery, use LARCHIVE or NBACKUP. In LARCHIVE, select Include All Directories and Exclude All Files. This process backs up the binderies and the trustee assignments in the directory structure, but does not back up the files. In NBACKUP, select Backup File Server, reply Yes to Backup Trustees, and enter ***.*** for Files to Exclude. This backs up the binderies and the trustee assignments but not the files. When you restore this backup to another server, all bindery information and trustee assignments are transferred.

Tech Tip: The structure of the bindery files was changed between NetWare 286 and NetWare 386. In NetWare 286, there are only NET$BIND.SYS and NET$BVAL.SYS. These files perform the same functions as the three bindery files in NetWare 386.

Why did the local paths set in AUTOEXEC.BAT disappear?

If you do not use MAP INSERT to map search drives in the system login script, these search drives will overwrite the first directories of your DOS path, instead of being inserted before your DOS path. The number of DOS path directories overwritten will correspond to the number of search directories mapped. If you have three directories set in your PATH statement and you have three search drives mapped in your login script, your DOS path will no longer exist, because it will have been completely overwritten by the network search path.

Tech Tip: In NetWare 386 there is a problem with the MAP S3:=*1: command. In NetWare 286 this command mapped a search drive to the first Novell drive map. With NetWare 386, this command gives the error "8998" during the login procedure. To solve the problem, place a period at the end of the command (following the colon).

What is the Service Advertising Protocol (SAP)?

The SAP enables servers to advertise their services to other devices on an internetwork. This advertising allows routers to keep a database of server data. Routers in turn transmit broadcasts to maintain synchronization among all routers on the internetwork. Workstations use SAP request packets to find servers. The time-synchronization feature uses SAP capabilities to communicate among single reference and primary time servers.

What are the 4.0 equivalents of CASTON and CASTOFF?

The following table lists the 4.*x* equivalents of CASTON and CASTOFF.

3.11	4.*x*
CASTOFF	SEND /A=C
CASTOFF ALL	SEND /A=N
CASTON	SEND /A

What is the 4.0 equivalent of SLIST?

NLIST SERVER /B is the 4.0 equivalent of SLIST in version 3.*x*. NLIST refers to all the NetWare 4.0 resources available. You must use the server switch to get a list of servers; otherwise, you get a list including many other items, such as directory, resources, username, and so on.

What is Large Internet Packet (LIP) and why is it significant?

Generally the size of packets that cross bridges or routers on NetWare networks is limited to 576 total bytes, although Ethernet and Token Ring are actually capable of carrying larger packets. LIP enables NetWare for the bigger packet sizes. This significantly increases throughput over bridges and routers (the larger the packet, the better the throughput). In NetWare 4.*x,* the workstation does not default to 576 bytes when a router is detected. Rather, it checks for the packet size supported by the router. LIP is enabled by default in the NetWare DOS Requester. Some old routers and bridges do not support LIP. It can be disabled by entering the following line in NET.CFG under the NetWare DOS Requester section heading:

```
LARGE INTERNET PACKETS = OFF
```

I'm running on thin Ethernet and getting a variety of serious errors such as file corruption, DOS critical errors, bad packets, and overall slow network performance. What's wrong?

Check your cabling. In a thin Ethernet, bus-topology network, so-called stub connections (that is, directly connecting a segment of Ethernet to the network card) can cause problems in signal phase, cable signal characteristics, and timing, all of which can wreak havoc on your network. The proper way to cable is to connect T connectors directly to your network interface card and connect the cabling through the Ts, as shown here:

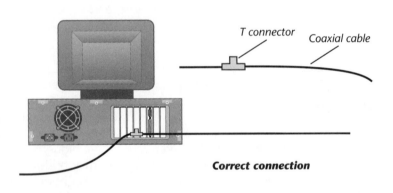

The following illustration shows the incorrect connection, in which there are extensions to the T connector:

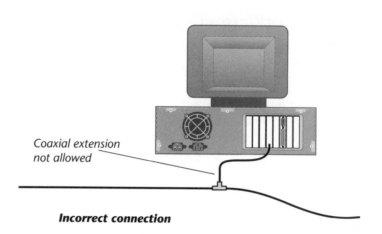

*Coaxial extension
not allowed*

Incorrect connection

Also, always be sure to properly terminate your network. Proper termination is crucial to the success of a thin Ethernet network. And check the cable length. Some other vendors have extended thin Ethernet specs, but they only work if every card on the network is from the same manufacturer. For example, thin Ethernet has a limit of 185 meters for 802.3 compliance, but 3Com claims to support 300 meters.

What are Novell's telephony services?

Novell's *telephony services* offer support for CSTA and for APIs written to the European Computer Manufacturers Association's CSTA standards. These standards enable computers to communicate directly to a PBX over the data network, instead of using a dedicated telephone. Automatic number identification, call reporting, and several other control features are available with telephony services, which include the following products: Client/Server API Suite, Telephony Server NLM, PBX Driver NLM, and PBX Link Hardware Driver NLM.

Initially, telephony services will handle call screening and routing. As standards are established in the future, telephony services and e-mail will probably merge. From their workstations, users will be able to browse both their e-mail and their voice mail and reply by either voice or text.

How does NetWare's file compression feature work?

File compression reduces the size of files that aren't being used and thus increases your available disk storage space. Users have the option of flagging specific files for compression. Compressed files are automatically decompressed when they are opened by a user.

TechTip: Novell recommends running file compression when the server is relatively idle.

File compression executes in the following steps:

1. Analyzes a file flagged for compression
2. Constructs a temporary file describing the original file
3. Checks to see if disk sectors will be saved by compressing the file
4. Constructs the compressed file
5. Swaps the original and compressed files after an error-free compressed version is constructed

---

NetWare 3.x

What are the main differences between NetWare 3.11 and 3.12?

Version 3.12 includes all patches and fixes that have been distributed for 3.11 since its introduction. In addition, 3.12 has the following enhancements:

- A simplified installation and menu system
- Bundling of five-user NetWare for Macintosh, MHS basic services, and e-mail
- Improved support for Windows
- Packet Burst support
- LIP support
- VLM client architecture
- Updated disk drivers; LAN drivers
- Improved utilities
- Improved file system, memory, and routing
- Standard Ethernet 802.2 frame support

- More efficient RIP and SAP code
- CD-ROM support

 I moved my workstation to a new location, and when I try to connect to the network I receive the error message, "A File Server Could Not Be Found." What does this mean?

Most likely, something is bad in the hardware connection between you and the server; this could involve the interface card, the cable, the connections, or the head end. First, go to the wiring closet and see if the new location is connected at all. If that's not the culprit, check the cable connection to the machine. If it's solid, the problem may be in the NIC. Attach a different machine to the cable, if possible—does the second machine work correctly? If so, the card in the first machine may be bad. If the second machine fails as well, you probably have a cable problem. (Time to get out the cable testers....)

 How can I tell what servers are available on the network?

Log in (or if you can't log in, load IPX and NETX), and get to a drive prompt. To see a list of NetWare file servers (copies of NetWare), type **SLIST**. To see a list of every IPX device that is broadcasting a name—including file servers and all other application servers, such as print servers, ACS, fax servers, and Named Pipes servers—go to the server console and type **DISPLAY SERVERS**. Note that viewing the list does not mean the services on it are available *to you*. To use a server on the network, you must either have an account on it or be able to log in or attach to it as GUEST.

Tech Tip: To see all network numbers, type **DISPLAY NETWORKS**.

When I log in, I get the error message, "Unknown File Server." What am I doing wrong?

You may be using the incorrect login format. The syntax for LOGIN is

LOGIN *server/user*

For example,

```
LOGIN SERVER1/JSMITH
```

Make sure that you haven't reversed the order of server and user. Also, make sure that you are typing the name of a valid server. Type **SLIST** to display a list of current NetWare servers.

How can I find a file on the NetWare 3.12 diskettes or CD-ROM?

Find the Install diskette, or the INSTALL directory on the CD-ROM. INSTALL contains a file called FILES.DAT, which lists all the files and their locations. You can search FILES.DAT with a word processor or text editor, and you can use NWXTRACT to extract the files.

How do I stop broadcast messages from going to my workstation?

At the DOS prompt, type **CASTOFF** or **CASTOFF ALL**. The CASTOFF command blocks messages from workstations, and CASTOFF ALL blocks messages from the server console in addition to workstations. CASTON restores broadcasts from all sources.

Tech Terror: When you suppress broadcast messages with either of these commands, you won't receive any system messages, regardless of their priority or importance. For example, you wouldn't want to miss "Server going down in 10 minutes!" Be careful—it can be painful to suppress messages as a rule.

What is the maximum password length in NetWare?

The maximum length for a password is 127 characters. While your own sense of security may be reinforced by the use of a long and cryptic password, you also have to remember it yourself, and type it every time you log in. In addition, keep in mind that NetWare provides the administrator the option to force users to change their passwords at regular intervals, and remembering a new password each time the old one expires can be complicated by longer and more complex usages.

What is intruder detection lockout, and do I need it?

Intruder detection lockout is a NetWare function that disables a user's account after a fixed number of unsuccessful login attempts (wrong password entered). The number of attempts is configurable. This feature is intended to stop anyone from determining a password by guessing at it again and again. If security is important to you, enable this feature.

Tech Terror: Be careful: If this feature is turned on for the supervisor account, you can be locked out of the system.

Why do my drive mappings disappear when I shell out to DOS from Windows?

Usually this is caused by selecting the incorrect shell version within Windows Setup. Check the version of NETX you are running (type **NETX I** from the command line). Check the version displayed against the version shown in Windows Setup. If the two are not the same, change the setting in Windows to reflect the version you are actually running.

It is possible to choose 3.26 in Windows even if an earlier version is running. In general, for Windows to utilize NetWare correctly, you want to run at least IPX 3.10 and NETX 3.26. The correct versions of NETX and IPX.OBJ files are included with Windows. For better Windows performance over the network, expand these files and regenerate the IPX for your workstation.

When I assign new drive mappings from a shell-out to DOS, why don't they appear when I return to Windows?

In order for these new mappings to appear, you must set the option for NetWare Share Handles to True in the Network Control Panel. Also, if you are in File Manager, you may need to refresh the screen.

Users are losing their connections, and the network is slow to respond. How should I begin to look for the cause of this problem?

You are probably either reaching the limits of your network topology, or there is a problem in your cabling plant. This is usually *not* a NetWare problem. The first issue to consider is whether changes have been made to the network. How many users are there on the segment where the problems are occurring? Have you added users or made the network larger? Did you attach the LAN to a WAN? What is the overall cable length on that segment? Are you using repeaters and, if so, how many? ARCnet, Ethernet, and Token Ring all have theoretical limits for overall cable length and maximum number of connections. As you begin to approach these thresholds, response can get flaky—not necessarily all at once and consistently, but intermittently. A bad cable or cable connection may also be the culprit. Are users connecting to a remote server by mistake? If you do not have a preferred server set in SHELL.CFG or NET.CFG, a user can attach to the first server that responds, which is sometimes a remote server. If none of these things has occurred to change the entire network map, you'll need to look for other things.

For instance, in 2.*x* versions your problems may be caused by the server running out of service processes. Version 2.15c cannot change the number of service processes available. Each VAP, print server, disk controller, or network adapter can use a file service process. When you run out of processes, the server quits accepting work and slows down. Connections may be dropped, and everyone sees the slowdown. You must have at least a single process available—which isn't really sufficient because it means the server can only process one request at a time. To get back more service processes, you must remove some resource, such as a printer, or reduce directory entries. Use the CONFIG utility at the server console to see how many service processes are in use and available. If necessary, increase the number of available service processes by unloading some VAPs. A better solution would be to upgrade to NetWare 2.2, in which ten file service processes are the default, and you will be able to configure more resources on the server.

In NetWare 386, look at the number of service processes available in the MONITOR utility. NetWare 3.11 and 4.0 both auto-tune this parameter and will set it up to 100 service processes. You probably do not want to force this number higher, because these processes use memory and can cause other performance problems.

What is the NetWare bindery? What files does it contain and what do they do?

The *bindery* is a database that contains definitions for objects such as users, passwords, groups, and workgroups. The three files that make up the bindery database are NET$OBJ.SYS, NET$PROP.SYS, and NET$VAL.SYS. They are hidden, flat database files that reside in the SYSTEM directory on the SYS: volume of a server.

- NET$OBJ.SYS is for objects. An *object* represents any physical or logical entity that has been given a name—for example, users, groups, and servers.

- NET$PROP.SYS is for properties. *Properties* are the characteristics of each object—for example, passwords, Internet addresses, group members, and account restrictions.

- NET$VAL.SYS is for *property data sets*, which are the actual values assigned to each object's properties.

When I run Windows, I see the error message, "System error: Cannot read from Device NETWORK." What does this mean?

This error can be caused by many things: an inoperative server, an IRQ conflict with the network card, a RAM or base I/O address conflict with the network card, Windows 3.0 (it requires a patch), or your temporary disconnection from the network (Windows is always looking for something in the background). If you are running Windows from the network, you can't recover from this problem without rebooting. When running Windows locally, there is a chance you can get some of your work back.

To check the IRQ and I/O base address settings, type **IPX I** in the directory where IPX is located. Make sure that no other devices are using the shared RAM ranges specified for IPX, and that your network card address has been excluded with EMM386.EXE to avoid conflicts with Windows. If you decide to change the network card settings, remember that you must generate a new IPX.COM with SHGEN or WSGEN.

Is an increase in the number of physical read/write errors and Hot Fix block indicators significant?

Normally, the values for physical read errors and physical write errors should be very low, or 0. When these numbers increase, there may be communication problems (bad connections) with the hard disk controller. An increase in Hot Fix blocks may indicate possible hard disk failure in the future. The Hot Fix area is good for a maximum of 512 blocks. Though you can assign a larger area, it is not advisable, since an excess number of errors probably indicates a bad disk. NetWare by default assigns 2% of the disk to the Hot Fix area.

Why is the number of redirected blocks increasing on my server's hard drive?

Increasing numbers of redirected blocks means that the NOS has attempted to write data to bad blocks on your server's hard drive. When blocks are identified as bad, the NOS marks them as such, and then writes its data to the Hot Fix area instead. Your disk may be going bad, so before you do anything else, make a backup quickly and verify it. Then try running VREPAIR to check the drive's integrity. Redirected blocks usually indicate problems with the hard drive and/or hard drive controller. Also, make sure that you are using the most current device driver for your hard drive; contact the manufacturer if there is any doubt.

How can I prevent users from accessing the server console even when they are in front of the server?

MONITOR.NLM 1.75 includes a fix to keep the console locked in MONITOR under all conditions. In addition, this version fixes a problem in previous versions that caused the following error on the server: "GPPE running process Monitor Background process." This error generally occurs when MONITOR is loaded for extended periods of time (30 days or so); the problem is caused by resource contention between the foreground and background processes of MONITOR. To receive MONITOR.NLM 1.75, download patch #1565 from the Corporate Software Electronic Services System bulletin board, or call Corporate Software's Product Support Hotline.

I am running Microsoft Windows on a NetWare 3.*x* file server and I see the error message, "User exceeded outstanding NCP directory search limit." What does this mean?

The default limit is 51, although the supported values are from 10 to 1,000. This error message occurs when a user searches more than the default number of directories (51) at a time. Normally, only one NetWare Core Protocol (NCP) directory search occurs at a time. However, applications that support multiple simultaneous outstanding directory-search operations may require that you increase this default. To do so, add the following line to AUTOEXEC.NCF on the server:

SET MAXIMUM OUTSTANDING NCP SEARCHES: *number*

What is the difference between connections and users on a server?

A connection to a server is established when a workstation or print server is attached, not when a workstation is logged in to the server. The connection

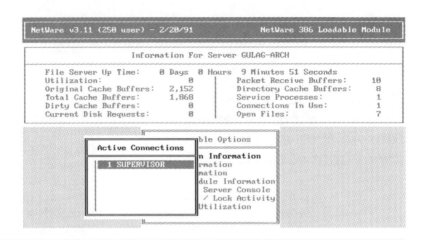

```
NetWare v3.11 (250 user) - 2/20/91          NetWare 386 Loadable Module

              Information For Server GULAG-ARCH

 File Server Up Time:     0 Days  0 Hours  9 Minutes 51 Seconds
 Utilization:                0    Packet Receive Buffers:   10
 Original Cache Buffers:  2,152   Directory Cache Buffers:   8
 Total Cache Buffers:     1,868   Service Processes:         1
 Dirty Cache Buffers:         0   Connections In Use:        1
 Current Disk Requests:       0   Open Files:                7
```

Active Connections

1 SUPERVISOR

ble Options

n Information
rnation
mation
dule Information
Server Console
/ Lock Activity
Utilization

FIGURE 2-2   Console MONITOR utility showing current connections

therefore occurs after the NetWare shell is loaded. The connection numbers that appear in USERLIST are issued in numerical order. Note that USERLIST is not an accurate check of connection information, because it checks for logins, not just attachments to a server. One way to check connection information is to run the MONITOR utility from NetWare, either from RCONSOLE or from the server console. At the main menu, Connections in Use is shown in the lower-right corner of the main menu, as shown in Figure 2-2. A single station can have more than one connection, as when you are running a print server in the background of a user workstation.

How can I determine which of two redundant routers is the primary one?

The one with the lower internal IPX number is the primary router because it occurs first in sequence on the routing table.

I just upgraded my network to 3.11, and users are getting this error message every time they try to log in: "Unknown error returned by attach (89fb)." Why?

Before performing an upgrade from NetWare 2.1*x* to NetWare 3.11, delete all user account passwords. Since the passwords are encrypted in NetWare 3.*x,* they cannot be transferred during the upgrade. (If you are upgrading from NetWare 2.0a, there is no need to delete passwords because the passwords are not encrypted.) After the upgrade is complete, reassign all user passwords. If you do not delete and reassign user passwords, users may receive the error message.

Where does NetWare store deleted files?

When files are deleted from a network volume, they are saved in a file on that volume and marked for deletion. They are then purged on a first-in/first-out basis so that they can be recovered by the SALVAGE utility. If, however, the directory that stores the deleted files is itself deleted, then the files are stored in a hidden directory on the root. This directory is called DELETED.SAV. Running the command CHKVOL on a server drive will tell you how many megabytes of deleted files are on the volume.

Where is the password for RCONSOLE set?

The RCONSOLE utility's password is actually set each time RCONSOLE.NLM is loaded. When loading RCONSOLE at the console prompt, type

LOAD RCONSOLE *password*

You can also put this line in the AUTOEXEC.NCF file so that it will load automatically when the server boots. The supervisor password or any other console operator password will also get you into RCONSOLE.

Tech Tip:
You cannot create subdirectories when using NetWare's RCONSOLE to transfer files to a subdirectory on a DOS partition. The directory must already exist; otherwise, the files are all copied to a file with the subdirectory's name.

Tech Tip: Be certain that you use NLMs, drivers, and other software utilities that are appropriate for your version of NetWare. These files are updated often, so check with NetWire frequently for current information. Whenever possible, use NetWare certified hardware. Off-beat products may promise some unusual functionality but may also bring with them the sort of intermittent problems that turn network administration into a nightmare.

How does the 4.0 version of RCONSOLE differ from the 3.11 version?

Enhancements to RCONSOLE in 4.0 include the following:

- It is now possible to encrypt the password required to access the server from a remote workstation. Rather than putting the password in AUTOEXEC.NCF you can use an encryption key instead of the password.

- Packet signatures are now required by default. This enables you to increase security when loading the RSPX module for direct remote-console connections. If you wish to disable packet signatures, enter the command **LOAD RSPX** with the SIGNATURES OFF parameter.

- Asynchronous connection options now allow you to set up a remote console session from a PC with a modem. A call-back parameter prevents unauthorized users from accessing the server via modem.

- The 4.0 version of RCONSOLE uses the following hotkeys:

Keystroke	Function
ALT-F1	Accesses the menu
ALT-F2	Quits the session
ALT-F3	Cycles backward through active screens
ALT-F4	Cycles forward through active screens
ALT-F5	Displays the workstation node address

When I come in to work in the morning, my workstation needs to be rebooted because its NetWare connection has been terminated. Is there anything I can do to prevent this?

Novell NetWare 3.11's security monitor, called *Watchdog*, runs at the server to disconnect idle connections to the server after a predetermined time. This means workstations with no packet activity over the network may lose their connections. Watchdog cannot be disabled, but you can set parameters at the server to delay the monitoring. The following SET parameters will delay the monitor for the maximum time (24 hours):

```
SET NUMBER OF WATCHDOG PACKETS = 100
SET DELAY BETWEEN WATCHDOG PACKETS = 10 MINUTES 26.2 SECONDS
SET DELAY BEFORE FIRST WATCHDOG PACKET = 20 MINUTES 52.3 SECONDS.
```

When I run NBACKUP, what does NetWare mean by the message, "Warning: Using Nbackup to restore to this version of NetWare may result in the loss of Non-DOS information"?

This message is misleading. What NBACKUP is really trying to tell you is that it has not detected any name space NLMs, such as MAC_NAM. Therefore, if you have saved any Macintosh, OS/2, or UNIX data to the file server, NetWare will not be able to save information such as the extended filenames and attributes. Files could be restored in the DOS eight/three format instead of the native format names.

Why can't I modify a file even though I have all effective rights in the directory?

Suppose you have a file that is owned by a specific user on the network, but many people have rights to use the file. If you delete the owner from the network, the file will appear to be Read Only to the other users. Users, including the supervisor, will be unable to make changes to the file. This problem can be corrected by changing the owner of the file or copying the file with another filename.

How does the workgroup manager function operate?

If you plan to employ the workgroup manager function in NetWare, you should start using it when you first set up your network. If you create users with supervisor equivalents, the workgroup manager will not be able to manage those users until you manually add the workgroup manager as a manager for them. Keep in mind that workgroup managers can only manage bindery objects that they create, and can only give object rights equal to their own.

I have noticed that the network adapter address in SESSION does not match the network address on my Lanalyzer monitor. What is happening?

The SESSION utility version 3.55 that shipped with NetWare 3.11 does not report node addresses correctly. If you select Session/Available Topics/User List, then choose a user and select Display User Info, the node address will be incorrect. Novell is aware of the problem and is working on a solution. In the meantime, you can either use an older version of SESSION or enter **USERLIST /A** for the node information.

Are there problems running the Edit NLM from 3.11?

The Novell NetWare 3.11 EDIT.NLM has a limitation that is not mentioned in the documentation. EDIT can only handle files that are 8K or smaller. If the file is larger, the editor will not load it. Also, the documentation for EDIT shows the use of forward slashes (/) when entering a filename, but that is wrong. You must enter backslashes (\).

How can I prevent users from logging in?

In version 3.1, you can disable logins for everyone except supervisor equivalents by typing **DISABLE LOGIN** at the file-server console prompt, or by using the Status option in FCONSOLE and changing the Allow New Users to Login setting to No. To disable logins for supervisor equivalents, set global time restrictions to make the current time unavailable to the group Everyone.

I have assigned a workgroup manager to manage a group, but the workgroup manager cannot change the user properties. What am I doing wrong?

Assigning a group to a user account manager allows the manager to manage only the properties of the group, not the properties of the users. To manage the properties of a group, the users of a group, or a combination of the two, the user account manager needs to be given the specific assignment as manager of the group, of the users, or both. Creating workgroup managers on a server can provide added security to the server and still allow multiple workgroups to operate on the same server, treating the server as if it were multiple servers. This hierarchical structure can be confusing, however, since groups and users are distinct.

NetWare 2.*x*

After upgrading to a new version of NetWare, I see less available memory when running Lotus 1-2-3. What has happened?

If you are using the MENU utility from NetWare 2.2 or NetWare 3.11, you may run out of memory. NetWare 2.2 and 3.11 both shipped with MENU.EXE and MENUPARZ.EXE files, version 2.30. This program combination takes far more RAM than the combination of MENU.EXE 1.23 and MENUPARZ.EXE 1.22. Newer MENU.EXE and MENUPARZ.EXE programs, version 2.31, use only 10K of memory. They are available from Corporate Software's Product Support Hotline as patch #1363.

Can I run NetWare 2.2 with DOS 5 or 6.*x*?

Yes. Check NetWire, NOVLIB 3, for a file called 22DOS5.ZIP. It contains the patch file ROMINT15.COM. This is necessary to run VREPAIR on either dedicated or nondedicated servers.

Servers and Server Installation

Server configuration and troubleshooting are the heart of network administration and are crucial to its health. New advances in CPUs can affect server performance dramatically, and changes on the server affect the entire network. As clock speeds in today's machines surpass 150 MHz, Novell's promise of 1,000 user licenses will become a reality; and as the user population approaches this new level, the need for network administrators and support personnel to have a comprehensive knowledge of server maintenance is even more critical than in the past. Gigabytes of storage space are no longer uncommon in LAN installations. Similarly, many of today's LAN environments have 32 to 64MB of RAM, and Intel Pentium-based computers promise access to substantially more. These progressive breakthroughs make it ever more important for the server to perform its daily tasks with dependability.

When considering the type of CPU you need for use as a file server, you should consider the issue of RAM versus CPU speed. If you have cost constraints, you might want to invest more heavily in server RAM. For example, a 33 MHz 486 CPU with 20MB RAM will outperform a 66 MHz Pentium CPU with only 8MB RAM when executing basic file and print services. Of course, if cost isn't a factor, it's best to invest in the fastest CPU available.

FRUSTRATION BUSTERS!

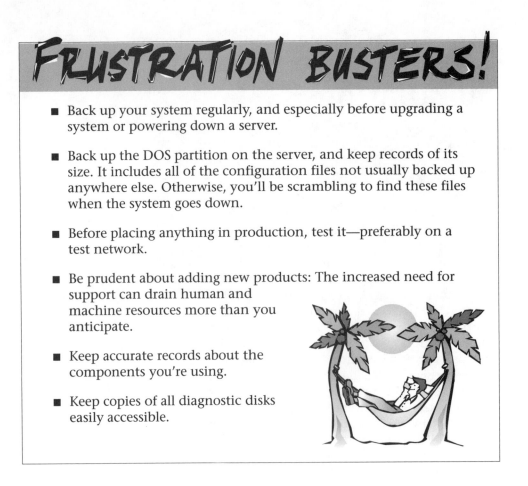

- Back up your system regularly, and especially before upgrading a system or powering down a server.

- Back up the DOS partition on the server, and keep records of its size. It includes all of the configuration files not usually backed up anywhere else. Otherwise, you'll be scrambling to find these files when the system goes down.

- Before placing anything in production, test it—preferably on a test network.

- Be prudent about adding new products: The increased need for support can drain human and machine resources more than you anticipate.

- Keep accurate records about the components you're using.

- Keep copies of all diagnostic disks easily accessible.

I installed a new file server and it won't communicate with the network wire. What's wrong?

There are lots of places to check for a problem. Is the cable firmly connected to the back of the machine? Is the correct driver loaded? Is the network card bad? Try replacing it with a card that you know is good and then see if you can connect. Are the settings on the card correct? Make sure that the network connection you are using is enabled on the card, for instance, BNC or RJ45. Many Ethernet cards are enabled by default for a BNC connection, but you might need to enable the setting for a twisted pair connection. Switch the card setting and try again.

Should I have an uninterruptible power supply (UPS) connected to my file server?

Yes. NetWare keeps a significant amount of data in cached RAM. A sudden power loss will result in lost data and damaged volumes. Any shared device that could lose data from a power surge should be protected with a UPS.

What are disk allocation blocks?

NetWare divides each volume into subdivisions called *disk allocation blocks*; these blocks can be configured as 4K (the default), 8K, 16K, 32K, or 64K. The allocation block size is set up when a NetWare partition is first created using INSTALL.NLM. NetWare stores files in blocks, and the size configured equals the minimum amount of space a file can occupy. If a file consists of more than one block, the file may be stored in adjacent or nonadjacent blocks. The DOS file allocation table (FAT) stores information on how to link the blocks together.

The configured block size can affect performance as well as the availability of disk space on the network, depending on the average file size used. For example, if you work with relatively small files (10 to 20K) and have limited space, you wouldn't want a 64K allocation block because this would waste considerable disk space. On the other hand, if you have a large disk drive (greater than 1GB) and you want to improve performance, a larger block size will help. The allocation block size must also be equal to or greater than the cache buffer size in order for a volume to mount; for example, a volume with allocation blocks of 4K will not mount if the cache buffer size is 8K.

What is the Original Cache Buffers value?

The Original Cache Buffers value is the number of cache buffers available when the file server is first booted. This can be seen in MONITOR at the main menu. The Original Cache Buffers value represents the number of blocks installed as memory in your file server, and is dependent on the total drive space and the amount of memory. For example, if you have a small drive and a large amount of memory—say, a 300MB hard disk and 12MB of RAM—you will have a relatively high number of cache buffers.

What is directory caching?

Directory caching allows you to store the file allocation table and directory entry table in RAM, to speed up file access. NetWare demands that disk volumes be cached, and warns if there is not enough memory to cache a volume.

What is elevator seeking?

Elevator seeking is a technique used to optimize disk reads. Current requests are queued based on the location of the data relative to the disk heads, not on the order in which they are received.

How do I get my server to recognize more than 16MB of memory?

Use the REGISTER MEMORY command at the system console. The syntax of this command is

REGISTER MEMORY *start length*

where *start* is the starting hexadecimal address of your 16MB (usually 1000000); and *length* is the hexadecimal length (or amount) of the additional memory you want your server to recognize. (There is a chart of the hexadecimal values for memory in the NetWare System Administration manual, File Server Utilities section, page 217.)

For example, to get your server to recognize 20MB of memory, use the following command:

```
REGISTER MEMORY 1000000 400000
```

Also, adding the following statement to the STARTUP.NCF will have the same effect of recognizing memory above 16MB:

```
SET AUTO REGISTER MEMORY ABOVE 16 MEGABYTES = ON
```

If you are using REGISTER MEMORY to register memory manually, and the file server still doesn't recognize any memory above 16MB, you could have a hardware problem. Using a Novell Certified EISA-based file server with a Novell Certified bus-mastering disk controller will provide the best support for utilizing RAM above 16MB. EISA machines will automatically register memory. If you have an ISA machine, then you must use a bus-mastering disk controller. At the server console, set this parameter:

```
AUTO REGISTER MEMORY = OFF
```

Also, be sure to use the most recent release of the driver for your controller.

If you're still having trouble, follow these steps:

1. Do not load any disk drivers in the STARTUP.NCF.

2. Copy the AUTOEXEC.NCF to the same directory on the server's DOS partition that contains SERVER.EXE and STARTUP.NCF.

3. Register memory in AUTOEXEC.NCF after the INTERNAL IPX NET entry.

4. Load the disk drivers; then mount the volumes.

This should allow all the memory to be recognized before any volumes are mounted.

Tech Tip: If you have a 32-bit machine (for example, a Compaq SystemPro) and wish to use superextended RAM (more than 16MB of RAM), all the boards in the machine must be 32-bit cards.

Tech Tip: If your file server has more than 16MB of memory and you are using an IBM Token Ring 16/4 Adapter/2 with on-line DMA, you might receive "abend" errors with a GPPE when loading TOKENBM.LAN. To fix this, add the following SET command to STARTUP.NCF and reboot the file server: "SET AUTO REGISTER MEMORY ABOVE 16 MEGABYTES = OFF." This will return the information message, "384K of memory will not be used," which means the file server has 384K of memory addressed above 16MB that will no longer be used.

 ## What does NetWare mean by the message, "Invalid request returned NPutIOCTL"?

This typically appears when you're running a machine with an Adaptec HA1540 controller card and more than 16MB of memory. Resolve the problem by adding the following statement to STARTUP.NCF:

```
SET AUTO REGISTER MEMORY ABOVE 16 MEGABYTES = OFF
```

Tech Tip: Some Adaptec 16-bit disk or tape SCSI controllers do not work properly with more than 16MB of RAM in the server.

 ## What is TAPEDAI.DSK?

TAPEDAI.DSK is a tape device driver designed to use the Advanced SCSI Programming Interface (ASPI). Novell ships this generic ASPI driver with NetWare 3.12 and 4.*x*. If you are using the CD, TAPEDAI.DSK is not copied from the CD to the server during installation unless it is selected as a disk driver at that time. If the installation is already complete and you need to use TAPEDAI.DSK, you can use NWEXTRACT (the Novell file decompression utility) to copy the driver from the CD. However, it is more common to use the device drivers that come with whatever SCSI controller you have.

When I load INSTALL.NLM and select Partition Tables from Disk Options, I get this message: "DOS 12 BIT FAT RELATIVE SECTOR...." What does this mean?

This happens when you are using an Adaptec 274x SCSI controller, and the EISA configuration setting EXTENDED TRANSLATION FOR DRIVES > 1 GBYTE is enabled. You must disable this setting if you are using this controller.

When I boot the server, I see the message, "Invalid Extended Directory Entry in FAT Chain." What does this mean?

This error usually indicates file system corruption. You can try to fix the problem with VREPAIR, but the prognosis isn't always good. You may need to delete the volume and then re-create it.

What does NetWare mean by the message, "IPX internal network number was NOT set"?

This typically occurs when you are booting the server. It means you have either specified an invalid number (only hexadecimal numbers are allowed for the internal network number), or entirely omitted the IPX INTERNAL NET line in AUTOEXEC.NCF (usually found after the file server name line). The syntax looks like this:

IPX INTERNAL NET *netnumber*

If I duplex the drives on my NetWare 3.*x* or 4.*x* file server, can I boot the server from the second drive of the pair if the first fails?

Yes, as long as you have a working DOS boot partition on both drives. After the primary drive fails, the duplexed drive becomes the primary one. Once you replace the failed drive with a new drive, mirror the existing primary back to that drive. When the image is complete on the new drive, force a shutdown on the existing primary drive to make the new drive become the primary. This may sound a little convoluted, but it's safer and more convenient than some of the alternatives, because you don't have to take down the server in order to make the replacement, and you don't move the only piece of equipment that has data on it until a mirror of it is in place. A schematic illustration of duplexing is shown here:

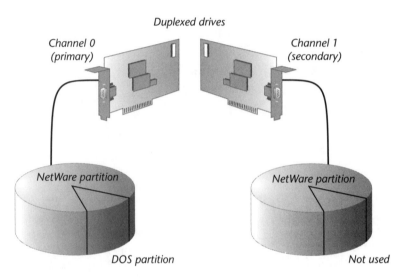

Duplexed drives

*Channel 0
(primary)*

*Channel 1
(secondary)*

NetWare partition

NetWare partition

DOS partition

Not used

Tech Terror: Be careful when you replace the failed drive because it is not primary, and if you remirror the drives the wrong way, you will wipe out the active primary drive. Make sure you have at least two current backups before you do anything!

Tech Tip: For the duplexed drive to boot properly, you may need to physically move it to the primary controller—depending on the controller you're using. Try to avoid this, because drives are sensitive to physical movement. It is never wise to disassemble a working component.

What does NetWare mean by the following message: "The mirror copies of the FAT don't match Volume SYS not mounted"?

By default, NetWare mirrors its FAT tables. When the server boots, it reads both FAT tables and compares them. If they don't match, the server will not mount the volumes. Possible causes of disparity include a bad driver, controller, or hard drive. To fix the problem, run VREPAIR or restore from a backup.

Tech Tip: Mirroring is defined by disk partitions rather than volumes. A disk partition defines the portion of the disk usable by NetWare and may contain more than one volume. Because a volume can be contained on multiple partitions, it is possible to mirror a disk that has part of a volume without mirroring the entire volume. For example, if drive 1 contains SYS and VOL1, and drive 2 contains more of SYS, drive 1 can be mirrored to a third drive without involving drive 2.

I entered a duplicate network number in AUTOEXEC.NCF, and errors appear every time I bring up the server. How do I correct my mistake?

First, if you don't know it, figure out what the correct entry is. Remember that there are two network numbers: the server number and the wire number. The wire number is used, for example, when you bind a driver, and must be the same on all the servers located on the same segment. The server number, on the other hand, must be unique. To see the server number of the current server, type **CONFIG** at the server console and then press ENTER. CONFIG returns the following statements:

FILE SERVER NAME *servername*
INTERNAL IPX NUMBER *ipxnumber*

The *ipxnumber* on the second line is the one that is currently running in the server; this is the one that must be unique (in hex) for each server.

If you are able to log in to the network in spite of the errors, SLIST will return the IPX number for *all* servers on the network.

Now that you know the numbers not to use, you have several choices about entering the new one:

- One alternative is to bring up the server with the errors it generates, immediately use LOAD INSTALL to edit the AUTOEXEC.NCF and correct the error, then bring down the server. When it comes back up, the problem will be corrected.

- Another choice is to bring up the server manually without executing AUTOEXEC.NCF. To do so, type **SERVER NA** at the DOS prompt. Once the server comes up, use LOAD INSTALL to edit the AUTOEXEC.NCF file, bring down the server, and bring it up again normally. The error will be corrected, and no errors will have been generated on the network while you were fixing the problem.

- The third alternative is to disconnect the server from the rest of the network, make the fix, and then restart.

 ## When the server crashes with a GPE error, Novell support tells me to "dump an image of server memory" and send it to them on a floppy. What does this mean?

NetWare allows you to dump an image of server memory to disk at the time of failure. This image can then be loaded onto systems at Novell in order to diagnose the cause of the server crash. If you're going to go through with this, dump to the DOS boot partition of the server. Although you can also dump to floppy disks, for 16MB of server memory you will need 15 floppies (3.5-inch, 1.44MB) and *lots* of time, and for a 40MB server, you'll need 35 floppies. What's more, it's almost a certainty that one of those floppies will turn up bad during the dumping process, causing you to lose the whole memory image. So you're better off dumping the image to the boot partition and copying it later to some media for transmission to Novell. Of course, you must have enough free space on the DOS partition to accommodate the image file, which could be as large as the total installed RAM in the file server.

Tech Tip: GPEs should not occur, and when Novell asks you to send them the memory image it is more for their benefit in searching for arcane NetWare bugs than for getting your system up and running. If you've got limitless time to help them, go ahead and spend the day copying to floppies. More than likely, if you just restart your server, everything will get back to normal, and the problem may not occur again. For future reference, try to remember to write down what events were happening at the time of failure. For example, was the GPE coincidental with the commencement of a backup? An SQL query? Loading an NLM? In the long run, this information will probably be more useful to you than waiting for Novell to call you back.

When I restart the server after a crash, I see the message, "Volume Segment Table Is Corrupt." What does this mean?

When a NetWare volume spans multiple physical disks, NetWare creates a volume segment table. There is no way to repair this table if it is damaged. Your only alternative is to delete the volumes, reinstall them, and restore the system from your backup.

This problem occurs very rarely and is usually symptomatic of a defective hard disk.

Tech Tip: An individual disk from a volume that spans disks cannot be restored, so if your server is configured this way, it is good practice to back up often. Better still, if your budget can handle it, duplex the drives.

Can I back up to a network drive using the backup program that ships with DOS 5?

No. The DOS 5 backup program cannot back up to a network drive. Use either of the Novell utilities, SBACKUP or NBACKUP, to back up a NetWare file server.

What does NetWare mean by the message, "Error reading executable file"?

This typically occurs when you are booting the server. It means a DOS error occurred while SERVER.EXE was loading. Either SERVER.EXE is corrupt, or the server's boot device has a physical problem. Whenever possible, boot the server from a DOS partition, because booting from a floppy disk may cause problems. SERVER.EXE is a large file (about 1MB) and does not hold up well on diskettes because of their "temporary" nature. Also, the floppy drive on a server is rarely used, so it may be full of dust.

What is STAT.NLM?

STAT.NLM is a management utility that records server resource utilization statistics. It can be loaded or unloaded from server RAM while the server is running. STAT can be loaded at the server console; or, if you want to run STAT every time the server is booted, you can put the following line in the AUTOEXEC.NCF file:

LOAD STAT

During boot-up I get the message, "Error initializing LAN driver: The server will be shut down." What does NetWare mean by this?

The driver you selected was not successful in initializing the LAN NIC in the server. Review your installation configuration. Make sure that the LAN NIC you installed matches the LAN driver specified during installation. Check interrupt and I/O settings. Ensure that the LAN NIC is firmly seated in the system board slot. If necessary, move the NIC to a different slot.

What does NetWare mean by the message, "This module is already loaded and cannot be loaded more than once."

This message occurs when you're trying to load an NLM. Some modules cannot be loaded more than once. Certain modules, such as LAN card drivers, can be loaded re-entrantly for multiple protocols, but generally this message means what it says. Consult the appropriate vendor to see if the module can be loaded more than once.

NetWare 4.x

What does NetWare mean by the following messages: "Error loading NETMAIN.IL$," "Cannot find file NETMAIN.IL$," and "Invalid version of NETMAIN.IL$"?

These messages may occur during a NetWare 4.0 CD-ROM installation, because both the CD-ROM and the hard drive on which NetWare 4.0 is installed are attached to the same controller. When the NetWare disk driver is loaded, the DOS driver is overwritten and the CD-ROM connection is lost. The NetWare 4.0 Release Notes describe six ways to work around this problem. You can find them in the \DOC\ENGLISH\NW40 \README directory on the 4.0 CD-ROM disk.

Can I run NetWare Loadable Modules (NLMs) in protected mode on the file server?

Yes. NetWare 4.x has server memory protection features that guard OS memory from corruption by unstable NLMs. These features ensure that your server will not be halted by an unstable, insufficiently tested third-party NLM. Memory protection allows you to run NLMs in a separate memory domain called OS_PROTECTED. After you have loaded an NLM in the OS_PROTECTED domain (ring 1, 2, or 3) and found the NLM to be safe, you can confidently load it into the OS domain (ring 0), where it can run most efficiently. (Ring 0 is the place that has a direct pipeline to the NetWare Core Protocol.)

How do I attach to my 3.11 server from my 4.01 server?

The command ATTACH is not supported in NetWare 4.*x*. To attach to a 3.11 server when you are logged in to a 4.*x* server, you must use the command

LOGIN *servername*/*username* /NS

The /NS switch logs you in to the specified file server without executing login scripts or logging you out of the servers to which you are currently logged.

Tech Tip: While ATTACH is no longer an external command, in NetWare 4.*x*, it can be executed in a login script, thereby allowing you to attach to a NetWare 3.11 server.

Can I mirror or duplex a drive that is utilizing NetWare 4.x's built-in compression?

Yes. The procedure for setting up the mirrored partitions is identical to that in 3.11, and can be found in the INSTALL program. Compressed drives operate the same as uncompressed ones.

Tech Tip: It is not possible to mirror a hard disk volume on a smaller secondary disk volume. The secondary hard disk volume can be the same size as or larger than the primary volume, although the installation program will reduce the size of a mirrored partition to equal the primary partition. To install a mirrored partition on a smaller secondary disk, back up the primary volume partition to a volume size no larger than the secondary disk, and then restore it. INSTALL.NLM can then create the mirrored partition.

Tech Tip: With NetWare 4.0, portions of a volume can be compressed by using the FLAG command. FLAG can be set per file, directory, or volume.

I'm upgrading my 4.0 server to 4.01. When I'm copying files, why do I get this message: "An error occurred while parsing file"?

Novell recommends upgrading from 4.0 to 4.01 using its INSTALL.BAT. Use the following procedure to avoid any trouble:

1. Bring down the server.
2. Log in to the drive where your CD-ROM is mounted, and change to the NETWARE.40\ENGLISH subdirectory.
3. Type **INSTALL**.

How do I change the license on a 4.0 server?

At the command line of the server, type **LOAD INSTALL -M**. NetWare will then prompt you to insert the disk with the new licenses.

NetWare 3.x

What are the physical limit specifications for NetWare 3.11?

NetWare 3.11 installed on a server can support the following thresholds:

Item	Maximum Limit
Users*	1,000
Local printers (shared by the network)	235
Print servers	16
RAM (per file server)	4GB
Disk space	32 terabytes
Concurrent files open	100,000
Disks per volume	32
Volumes per server	64

*NetWare is sold in various user-license increments. This number is based on the license purchased, and 250 is the most common number. The 1,000-user version has never been in wide distribution.

I have a 100-user version of NetWare 3.11, but I want 150 users to have access to my file server. Can I buy an additional 50-user license and add it to my existing 100-user license?

Unfortunately, no—NetWare does not allow you to combine licenses. You must upgrade to the next level (250). However, the NetWare license is for *concurrent use* of the server. You can add more than 100 users to the bindery without upgrading, as long as no more than 100 connections are using the server at a given time. Remember that print servers and some NLMs also use a connection.

I'm upgrading my NetWare 3.11 server to version 3.12, and NetWare won't accept the path I enter, even though it is correct. What's wrong?

Check to see if you are mistyping the path. If that's not the problem, you are probably loading the old INSTALL program from 3.11. This is dated August 2, 1993, and the problem has been fixed by an update from August 17, 1993.

To ensure that you are using the right version, copy INSTALL.NLM to your DOS partition from the 3.12 floppy, and then run it by typing **LOAD C:\INSTALL.NLM** at the command line. Once the program has started, check the version at the top of the screen. It should read "NetWare 3.12 Install." The correct version for 3.12 installation is 1.57. This number should also appear at the top of the screen.

Two subdirectories reference the same first directory block. What should I do?

Your server may have experienced a power surge or other problem that has damaged files on its primary volume. Run VREPAIR to rectify this condition. Dismount the volume at the console prompt, and then enter the command

VREPAIR *volumename*

at the command line.

When I try to load SERVER.EXE on a file server with 16MB RAM, why do I see the message, "Insufficient memory to run NetWare 386"?

This appears if you have DOS loaded high. Avoid loading DOS (or any other TSR) high, and SERVER.EXE should be able to allocate enough memory for itself. The best approach is simply to avoid loading the HIMEM.SYS device driver in your CONFIG.SYS. It serves no useful purpose on a NetWare file server. In fact, there is seldom a need for a CONFIG.SYS at all.

How do I install a user upgrade diskette?

Replace the SERVER.EXE file on the server, with the new one on the user upgrade diskette. This file contains the serial number and the user license information.

During a NetWare 3.11 installation on a Zenith 386/33 with a DTC hard drive controller, INSTALL.NLM crashes at the Partition option. What should I do?

Load ISADISK with the /b parameter to stop the server from crashing. The /b flag forces the ISADISK driver to act like the 3.10 ISADISK driver, and checks the BIOS for drive information.

I just installed NetWare 3.12 on Ethernet. I've checked the cabling and the card in the server, and both seem fine, but all workstations get the error, "File Server Not Found." What's wrong?

You probably have the wrong Ethernet frame type established. NetWare 3.12 defaults to using Ethernet frame type 802.2. (NetWare 3.11 used 802.3.) Changing the frame type in the AUTOEXEC.NCF to 802.3 should solve the problem. To do so, edit the line that loads your LAN driver in the AUTOEXEC.NCF by changing the frame type to Ethernet_802.3; for example,

```
Load Ne2000 Port=300 Int=e Frame=Ethernet_802.3
```

Alternatively, you can install the new ODI drivers on your workstations. These use 802.2 as the default.

Why isn't HELP available after I install NetWare 3.12?

Starting in version 3.12, NetWare Help is provided by an interactive program called *Electrotext*. This program is shipped with the CD-ROM packages but must be ordered separately if you've purchased the floppy disk version. To purchase Electrotext, call this toll-free number: 800-336-3892.

How do I upgrade from a NetWare 3.11, 50-user server license to a NetWare 3.11, 100-user server license?

Bring down the server, and replace SERVER.EXE with the new version of the file that is on the System_1 diskette of the upgrade. SERVER.EXE resides in the DOS partition of the server.

Tech Tip: Make sure you have a full backup of the entire system before attempting an upgrade.

Can I upgrade from NetWare 2.2 to NetWare 4.0?

Yes. The NetWare 4.0 installation utility allows this upgrade.

Can I use the MIGRATE utility to upgrade from NetWare 3.11 to NetWare 3.12?

Yes. Novell recommends using the MIGRATE utility over all other alternatives.

I upgraded my CPU from a 386 to a 486 and installed the hard drive from the old machine. When I try to run SERVER.EXE, it abends and displays "Abend: Improper ROM parameter." What's wrong?

Make sure that the hard drive type you have selected in your BIOS is correct. Various machines often use different numbers for the same drive type; or you may have selected a drive type that appears to have the correct number of cylinders and heads, but it isn't the proper one.

What is the runtime version of NetWare 3.x?

The "runtime version" of NetWare 3.x is a reduced version of the full operating system; this version does not contain file or print services. It allows you to set up additional servers dedicated to specific tasks, such as backup or communications, thereby removing processing overhead from the main file server. Intel's Backup Server, and ORACLE for NetWare are both examples of runtime NetWare systems.

Why is the server time incorrect after I bring down the server and restart without rebooting?

NetWare sets the system clock at boot-up by getting the current time from CMOS. From then on, it keeps the time using a software clocking algorithm and gets the ticks for its system clock from the timer chips on the system board. When the file server switches into real mode, however, it stops keeping time and depends on DOS to keep the system time. After switching back to protected mode, NetWare continues where it left off, rather than updating the time. This can cause discrepancies in the system time.

An NLM called SYNCTIME, which synchronizes the system time on a file server, is available for NetWare 386 3.1. To receive this NLM, download patch #1539 from the Corporate Software Electronic Services System bulletin board, or call Corporate Software's Product Support Hotline.

I'm trying to load the hard disk driver for my server, and NetWare insists that the file does not exist, even though it is in my DOS partition. What's wrong?

If the driver is located in the DOS partition of your server, try typing **LOAD** *D:\filename.***DSK** (where *D* is the location of the file) at the command line. If that doesn't work, check the attribute of the file. NetWare seems to be incapable of seeing files in the DOS partition that are marked as Read Only. If the file is marked RO, you can remove the attribute with the following command:

ATTRIB -R *filename*.DSK

For a Hot Fix area, what is the largest percentage of disk space I can use?

The default for a Hot Fix area is 2% of disk space. However, the percentage is less important than the actual size of the Hot Fix area. The maximum size is 30,720 blocks or 125MB, but if you need this much space, the disk is almost certainly bad.

How do I remove name space from a volume?

The only way to remove name space from a volume is to run VREPAIR from the server console.

How do I determine the amount of memory required by my server?

For each DOS volume, use the following formula:

(.023 x (volume size in MB)) / block size of volume (4K to 64K)

For each volume with name spacing, use the following formula:

(.032 x (volume size in MB)) / block size of volume

Add the totals of the formulas, plus 4MB for the operating system, and round up to the nearest megabyte.

This formula does not provide an exact figure, but it does give you a good estimate of the amount of memory required if you use the server for file and print services only. The minimum amount of memory required for a NetWare server is 4MB. If the total from either of the above formulas is less than 4MB, use 4MB. NLMs require additional memory. Consult the appropriate manuals to check individual requirements for specific applications.

Tech Tip: The foregoing calculation provides information for only a vanilla installation of NetWare, essentially computing the memory needed to cache directory tables for the disk drives. The calculation assumes no extraordinary overhead or processes; for example, it tells you nothing about actual requirements if you are loading GMHS or a SQL server.

How do I stop the server from making a backup copy of every file I delete from the server?

At the server console, enter the following command:

```
SET File delete wait time = 0
```

Tech Terror: Once this parameter is set, you will not be able to recover files using the SALVAGE utility.

How do I determine the correct packet size for a token ring network?

There are multiple factors to consider in configuring token ring file servers and workstations to an appropriate packet size (sometimes called frame size). In general, the larger the packet size, the faster the transmission of data over the wire. This is balanced by the fact that the larger packets place a greater burden on the file server's capacity and performance. Packet size is also limited by the token ring hardware in use.

The following maximum packet sizes appear in IBM's LAN Administrator's Guide:

Adapter	Speed	Packet Size
IBM 16/4 Mbps Adapter	16 Mbps	8,144 bytes
IBM 16/4 Mbps Adapter	4 Mbps	4,472 bytes
IBM TR 4 Mbps Adapters	4 Mbps	2,052 bytes

The server is capable of maintaining simultaneous sessions with workstations using different packet sizes. In other words, one workstation communicating with 512-byte packets will not force all communications to 512-byte packets. The server will individually negotiate a maximum packet size for each workstation equal to the smallest defined packet size for each server/workstation pairing. This is how a workstation with a 2K packet can communicate with a server with 1K packets.

Certain limits do apply. An IBM Token Ring Adapter II, with its maximum packet size of 2,052 bytes (2K), cannot negotiate with a packet any larger than this. Therefore, a server with an Adapter II communicating with a 1K packet cannot negotiate a common packet size with a workstation communicating with a 4K packet. Even though the ATTACH and LOGIN commands can execute, data transmission to the server will be truncated to 1K. If the packet size of the workstation is set to 2K (IPX o,tbz=2048), then successful negotiation (to a 1K packet size) can take place. If possible, it is advisable to establish a standard packet size on all machines on the ring.

How do I configure two IBM Token Ring adapters on a NetWare 386 server?

When you configure two IBM Token Ring cards in a server, the selection of options 0 and 2 will fail. With NetWare 386 3.0, you receive an error such as "Token Ring adapter did not exist at port A24." With NetWare 386 3.1, you receive an error such as "ERROR: frame type is already loaded." Use the following tested configuration:

```
LAN A:
IRQ=2
ROM=CC00
RAM=D800
```

(Switch #9 should be set to off. This selects the primary card.)

```
LAN B:
IRQ=3
ROM=C800
RAM=D400
```

(Switch #9 should be set to on. This selects the alternate card.)
Then, in AUTOEXEC.NCF, enter the following LOAD statements in place of the current ones:

```
LOAD TOKEN PORT=A20
LOAD TOKEN PORT=A24
```

You do not need to specify the port for the first LOAD statement, but it is required for the second one. Also, COM2 must be disabled, because it uses IRQ 3. Figure 3-1 shows the switch settings for the IBM Token Ring Adapter II.

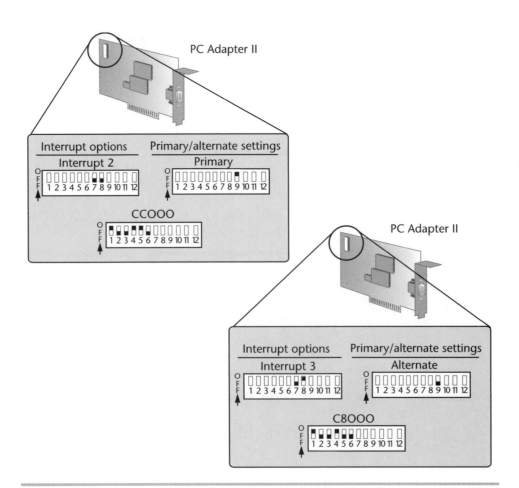

FIGURE 3-1 Switch settings for the IBM Token Ring Adapter II

How does data migration work on a server?

In NetWare 4.0, data migration is set by volume, not by directory. For example, if the volume is 80% full, NetWare begins migrating the least-recently-used data until the volume is 70% full.

Why can't I access my 3.11 server when my 4.*x* server is unavailable?

This is part of the "transition phase" that Novell is making everyone endure. The new IEEE Ethernet standard is 802.2, and Novell wants you to use it. Beginning with the latest ODI drivers and NetWare 3.12, NetWare defaults to 802.2. If you need 802.3 or Ethernet type II (NetWare 3.11), you must specify it in the server's startup AUTOEXEC.NCF and/or the workstation NET.CFG. If you can use a workstation to attach to a NetWare 3.11 server through a NetWare 4.0 server using VLMs, but you cannot log in to the NetWare 3.11 server when the NetWare 4.0 server is unavailable, check the NET.CFG file. The 802.3 frame type probably is not specified in the file. When VLMs are used to log in to a NetWare 4.0 server and then attach to a NetWare 3.11 file server, the NET.CFG on the workstation should list both frame types, with 802.3 listed first. For example, the NET.CFG file would look like this:

```
Link Driver XXXXXXXX
Frame Ethernet_802.3
Frame Ethernet_802.2
```

It is important to set 802.3 first. If both frame types are used when loading and binding each server's LAN cards, no frame type statements need to be added to the NET.CFG file.

What does NetWare mean by the message, "VLM.EXE file is using extended memory (XMS)"?

This appears when VLMs are loading, regardless of whether they occupy upper memory blocks or conventional memory. Extended memory (XMS) occupies physical memory locations that DOS can access only through a memory manager. Although most VLMs are loaded into XMS memory, a small window (approximately 46K) is opened in memory below the 1,024K boundary. By default, VLM.EXE tries to put this in the upper memory blocks; otherwise, it is placed in conventional memory.

You can confirm memory usage by using the DOS MEM command before and after the VLMs have loaded. For example, the command MEM /C More displays a list of all TSRs loaded in memory.

After installing the VLMs on a workstation, my shared copy of Windows won't load. Why?

This can occur if you are running a network version of Windows and you install the VLMs and NetWare 4.*x* support in a shared directory on the network. Until all workstations are upgraded, workstations running NETX will receive a number of errors that can cause Windows not to load.

To solve this problem, download patch #1577 from the Corporate Software Electronic Services System bulletin board, or call Corporate Software's Product Support Hotline. If you download patch #1577, continue by creating a subdirectory in the network WINDOWS directory. Into the subdirectory, copy the VIPX.386 and VNETWARE.386 files from the WINUP7.ZIP file contained in patch #1577. Edit the [386 Enh] section of each workstation's SYSTEM.INI file to reflect the new path for VNETWARE.386, VIPX.386, and NETWARE.DRV, as in the following example:

```
NETWORK=F:\WINDOWS\NEW\VNETBIOS
F:\WINDOWS\NEW\VNETWARE.386
F:\WINDOWS\NEW\VIPX
```

What does NetWare mean by the following messages: "Call to undefined Dynalink" and "You are not logged in to Directory Services. You must be logged in to Directory Services before you can run NETADMIN. The current operation cannot be completed"?

If you are still using IPX and NETX instead of VLMs, you will see one of these error messages when you're logged in to a NetWare 4.0 server: If you are running NWADMIN, the Dynalink message will appear. If you are running NETADMIN, the Directory Services message will appear.

You must use VLMs in order to be able to access NDS. Run the client installation for NetWare 4.0 that provides new drivers for DOS and Windows. These drivers allow you to log in as an authenticated user and perform NDS administration using NWADMIN or NETADMIN.

Tech Tip: If you plan to use the maximum dirty disk cache delay in the server's AUTOEXEC.NCF, make sure you set it after loading all the NLMs. If you set the dirty disk cache delay before the MONITOR.NLM or any of the other NLMs are loaded, the server may hang. If you increase the dirty disk cache delay, the server's performance will improve because the directory tables will be held in cache longer. The trade-off is that directory tables may not be written to disk in time and they can become corrupted. The default delay setting is .5, and it can range from 0 to 10. For example, the following sets the delay to the maximun value:

```
SET DIRTY CACHE DELAY TIME = 10
```

Where is the serial number for my copy of NetWare stored?

NetWare 386 is serialized in SERVER.EXE, not on the Gendata disk as in NetWare 286. This information may be useful if you receive an error such as "Abend: File Server Not Serialized" when loading NetWare 386. This error usually occurs when SERVER.EXE is corrupted. If you suspect that SERVER.EXE is corrupted, recopy the file from the original disk.

What happens when I use SECURE CONSOLE?

If SECURE CONSOLE is invoked at the file server in NetWare 386, it removes DOS from memory, as if you used the REMOVE DOS command. The file server uses DOS in debug mode to locate devices. Therefore, if the file server goes into debug mode, you cannot do a system dump because the server cannot see a floppy drive.

What is SPEED?

NetWare provides a command called SPEED that you can use to display the speed at which a processor is running. When the server is booted, NetWare clocks the time of the processor. This information is then stored in a pool. To view the processor speed, type **SPEED** at the file server console.

The processor speed rating is determined by the following:

- CPU clock speed (such as 16 MHz, 20 MHz, 25 MHz)
- CPU type (such as 80386SX, 80386, 80486)
- The number of memory wait states (such as 0, 1, 2)

For example, an 80386SX CPU running at 16MHz should get a rating of about 95. An 80386 CPU running at 16MHz should get a rating of about 120, and a 486DX2/66 should get 900. If your computer has a slower rating than you expected, check the CPU speed setting.

All users suddenly lost their connection to the network. The file server keyboard does not respond. After bringing down the server, it displays the error message, "1790" in the upper-left corner of the console. What's wrong?

A "1790" message indicates that a disk drive has failed. Replace the disk drive, and restore data from your backups.

Can the Adaptec 154X SCSI controller be used for a disk drive and tape drive simultaneously?

No; this causes a conflict between the devices. You can, however, install multiple controllers in the server, one for each device.

Are there any special problems with the Adaptec 154XC adapter?

The Adaptec 154XC adapter sometimes causes drives that are attached to external subsystems to deactivate. A problem with this host adapter's external port causes the adapter to operate unreliably with some high-quality (low-density) SCSI cables. To fix this problem temporarily, use an Amphenol 10599 external low-density SCSI cable. Adaptec is working to resolve this issue in later versions of the 154XC adapter.

I'm using a Proteon NIC with a Proteon 4.06 driver. Why does my server abend or slow down the network when I reboot my workstation?

The Proteon 4.06 driver is defective. Obtaining driver 4.07 will fix the problem. Apparently the 4.06 driver did not close the connection correctly, causing corrupt packets to be sent out over the LAN.

How can I mount a CD-ROM drive on my server?

Both NetWare 3.12 and 4.0 now support CD-ROM drives as volumes. To install one, you'll need the drive, a SCSI controller, and a SCSI terminator. Follow these steps:

1. Load the driver for the controller.
2. Load the ASPI layer, unless it is loaded automatically by the controller's driver.
3. Load CDNASPI.DSK for a generic controller, or ASPICD.DSK if you are using an Adaptec controller.
4. Load CDROM.NLM.
5. At the file server, issue the following command:

    CD MOUNT *volume name* [or] *device number*

    You should now be able to map the CD-ROM as a network drive.

In NetWare 4.x, which CD-ROM formats are supported by CDROM.NLM?

This NLM supports ISO 9660 and High Sierra formats.

When mounting my CD-ROM as a volume in NetWare 3.12, is there a way to name the volume as something other than the volume label of the actual CD that is in the drive?

No. At this time, there is no way around this.

Why am I getting periodic parity errors on my server?

This usually indicates a memory error. If the parity error message includes a number, write it down. Look in your computer's installation manual or memory adapter's manual to see if you can determine which part of memory has failed. A diagnostic program such as CHECKIT! can help determine the location of the faulty memory and save you time and money, because you'll know right away which failed memory module you need to replace.

When writing large files to disk, my server abends and displays the error message, "Lost secondary interrupt." What's wrong?

This is sometimes caused when a machine that has bus mastering is used with an older 3C507 board. Older 3C507 boards do not work well on machines with bus mastering when the adapter and the disk need to be accessed at the same time. To rectify this situation, you need 3C507 boards that are revision 6750-11 or newer (for the DIX/BNC board) or revision 7508-04 or newer (for the TP board).

What is a packet receive buffer?

A *packet receive buffer* is an area in the file server memory that is set aside to temporarily hold packets arriving from various network workstations. The packets remain in this buffer until the file server is ready to process them and send them to their ultimate destination on the network. This ensures the smooth flow of data into the file server, even during times of particularly heavy I/O.

Tech Terror: In STARTUP.NCF, if you set Minimum Packet Receive Buffers to a number higher than 100 and do not set Maximum Packet Receive Buffers to a number higher than 300, you should expect a 20% to 30% reduction in file-copying performance to a server. In general, whenever Minimum Packet Receive Buffers is set significantly higher than Maximum Packet Receive Buffers, the system will drop packets. This statistic can be observed through the MONITOR screen under the LAN information section. Make sure that you set the Maximum number at least 200 higher than the Minimum number.

Why do I reach the Maximum Packet Receive Buffers limit? This has never occurred before, but now it happens very quickly after bringing up my server.

You can increase the Maximum Packet Receive Buffers setting by issuing the following statement at the console command line:

SET Maximum Packet Receive Buffers=*xxx*

If this doesn't do the trick and all other settings in AUTOEXEC.NCF check out, hitting the limit is probably caused by bad cabling or a bad network card. Try to isolate which segment of your network is causing the trouble, and then troubleshoot it further by replacing cabling, cards, or both.

How can I increase the Minimum Packet Receive Buffers limit?

From the file server console, type **LOAD INSTALL** to start the INSTALL utility. Select System Options, and then the Edit STARTUP.NCF File option. This displays the file in edit mode. Add the following line:

SET Minimum Packet Receive Buffers=*xxx*

where *xxx* is a number within the range 10 to 1,000. This parameter can only be set through STARTUP.NCF. For the command to take effect, you must bring the server down and reboot it. Be sure to type all parts of the SET command accurately, including the parameter and the value. For example,

```
SET ALLOW UNENCRYPTED PASSWORDS = ON
```

will work, but

```
SET ALLOW UNENCRYPTED PASSWORD = ON
```

won't.

When I load certain NLMs, the Total Server Work Memory displayed in MONITOR decreases by a multiple of 16 bytes. Does this mean that memory is lost when NLMs are loaded?

No. This number reflects the way that MONITOR.NLM calculates the amount of free memory. The Non-Movable Cache, Movable Cache, and File Cache totals all show the total allocated memory, including the overhead needed to manage these pools. However, the totals for Permanent and Alloc only reflect memory usable by an application and do not account for the overhead involved in managing the memory itself. So, anytime an NLM requires more memory, the server needs to move memory from file cache buffers to the Permanent pool. A full buffer (including overhead of 16 bytes) is taken from the file cache total. The usable memory added to the Permanent total is 16 bytes smaller because of the overhead. What this all amounts to is just a quirk in the way MONITOR.NLM calculates the totals. Keep in mind, though, that when NLMs are loaded they do use up server RAM. MONITOR.NLM happens to incorrectly report the total amount of fixed RAM installed in the server when certain NLMs are loaded.

When i upgraded a 3.11 server from PS2SCSI.DSK to PS2OPT.DSK, NetWare displayed the message, "DOS Partition Relative Sector *XX* And Size *XXXX* Do Not Match The Ending Cylinder *XX*, Head *XX*, Sector *XXX*." What does it mean?

This error message occurs when PS2SCSI.DSK and PS2OPT.DSK recognize the same drive with different geometric parameters. To solve the problem, follow these steps:

1. Back up the system.
2. Delete the NetWare partition created with the PS2SCSI.DSK driver.
3. Use the PS2OPT.DSK driver to re-create the NetWare partition.
4. Restore the system from the backup you ran in step 1.

Why is the UNICODE diskette hanging the 3.12 installation of SYSTEM and PUBLIC files?

The installation is probably not hanging at all. However, the UNICODE diskette takes so long to install that the system usually seems to have frozen. The UNICODE diskette includes 141 files that are copied to the following directories during installation:

SYS:SYSTEM\NLS
SYS:LOGIN\NLS
SYS:PUBLIC\NLS

If you are using DR DOS version 6.0, loading these files takes about 50 minutes. Other versions of DOS require less time.

How can I view the file server error log?

You must have Supervisor privileges in order to view the file server error log. Be sure to check the error log occasionally, even if you are not having problems with the system. Use the following procedure:

1. Run SYSCON.

2. From the main menu, choose Supervisor Options.

3. From the Supervisor Options menu, choose View File Server Error Log, as shown here, to view the log:

```
┌─Available Topics──────┐
│                       ║
│┌Accounting│┌──────Supervisor Options──────────┐
││Change Cur││                                   │
││File Serve││ Default Account Balance/Restrictions│
││Group Info││ Default Time Restrictions         │
││Supervisor││ Edit System AUTOEXEC File         │
││User Infor││ File Server Console Operators     │
│└──────────┤ Intruder Detection/Lockout        │
│           │ System Login Script               │
│           │ View File Server Error Log        │
│           │ Workgroup Managers                │
│           └───────────────────────────────────┘
```

You can move through the log by pressing CTRL-PGUP and CTRL-PGDN.

Login Scripts

What can we say? It's a fact of life: To do much of anything on the network, you have to log in.

In versions 3.12 and below, the *system login script* on the server is used to create systemwide login assignments. These are executed by every workstation when connecting to the server. Drive mappings, environmental variables, critical programs such as virus scanning software, important system messages, and other important settings are established for all network users in the system login script. *User login scripts*, on the other hand, allow you to tailor the environment for certain individuals.

Beginning with version 4.*x,* there are three types of login scripts: container, profile, and user.

FRUSTRATION BUSTERS!

- Always create a backup copy of the system login script, especially if you or other supervisors experiment with it. The system login script is called NET$LOG.DAT and is stored in the SYS:PUBLIC directory.

- Remember to use MAP DISPLAY ON and MAP ERRORS ON if you're trying to debug a login script. Setting these toggles to OFF suppresses the results from a login script—which is fine once things are working well. You'll want to turn them ON, however, when you're troubleshooting.

- If possible, avoid running TSRs from a login script.

- The search drives mapped in the system login script overwrite the local path set in AUTOEXEC.BAT on the boot device for a workstation. Be sure to reestablish a path to the necessary resources through the search drive mappings.

- Don't nest too many IF statements in a login script or the script might be difficult to debug. There are no debugging or error checking tools for the LOGIN utility, and you can waste unnecessary time trying to fix a procedure that you could better implement through another utility.

My login script aborts before I'm able to access any network drives. What's wrong?

If you are using any multi-line IF/THEN statements in your login scripts, make sure that you close each IF/THEN with an END statement, as shown in Figure 4-1. If you forget to terminate the conditional with END, the server will dump you from the login script. When this happens, you may not have sufficient rights or

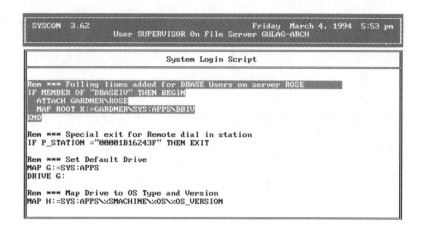

```
SYSCON  3.62                                 Friday  March 4, 1994  5:53 pm
                  User SUPERVISOR On File Server GULAG-ARCH

                             System Login Script

Rem *** Folling lines added for DBASE Users on server ROSE
IF MEMBER OF "DBASEIV" THEN BEGIN
  ATTACH GARDNER\ROSE
  MAP ROOT K:=GARDNER\SYS:APPS\DBIV
END

Rem *** Special exit for Remote dial in station
IF P_STATION ="00001B16243F" THEN EXIT

Rem *** Set Default Drive
MAP G:=SYS:APPS
DRIVE G:

Rem *** Map Drive to OS Type and Version
MAP H:=SYS:APPS\%SMACHINE\%OS\%OS_VERSION
```

FIGURE 4-1   A sample IF/THEN/END statement in a login script

drive mappings to perform any network functions. Also, make sure there's no EXIT command at the start of the login script, because EXIT stops any further processing of the login script and returns you to a command prompt.

Tech Tip: If the error message, "Invalid exit command followed by a string is not supported on this machine" appears when a user tries to log in to the network, edit the system login script and precede the EXIT line with the PCCOMPATIBLE command.

Why does NetWare display the message, "Batch File Missing" whenever I log out?

The batch file probably has no end-of-file marker in it. You can avoid this by adding the end-of-file marker (^Z) on the last line in the batch file.

You may also want to have the batch file set your default drive to the boot device before logging out. Then the current drive will always be local, and therefore always available. You can do this by having a batch file execute at startup, as the last line in the login script. For example, the last line of the login script might read:

```
EXIT "STARTUP"
```

Then STARTUP.BAT would have as its last lines:

```
C:
OUT.BAT
```

and OUT.BAT would need to be on the C: drive and contain the command LOGOUT.

How do I edit the default login script?

You cannot edit the default login script. However, the system login script will supersede the default login script, so use the system login script to establish common user parameters, and suppress the default login script through the EXIT or NO_DEFAULT statement. This prevents any other commands from executing within other login scripts.

What does NetWare mean by the message, "Your login script file has been locked too long by another station"?

This tells you that another user, probably the network administrator, is currently editing your login script file with a tool other than SYSCON (such as a text editor). This keeps the file open, and it is therefore not available to you. You cannot open the file when you log in, so NetWare executes the default login script instead. To prevent this situation from occurring, the network administrator should use the login script editor built into SYSCON, which edits a temporary copy of the file, but leaves yours available. The only limitation to this is that SYSCON allocates a 16K buffer and cannot handle edit files that are larger than 16K. If your system login script must be larger, use a different text editor to edit the file.

How do I prevent the default login script from executing?

There are several ways to deal with this problem. The default login script will not execute if a user login script exists. If you don't have a user login script, you can create one that does nothing except replace the default script. In the user login script, just enter a single line that says **EXIT**.

Version 3.65 of LOGIN.EXE allows the use of the NO_DEFAULT parameter in the system login script. This inhibits the execution of the default login script. After NetWare reads the system login script, it looks for a user login script. If none is present, NetWare runs the default script, unless NetWare encounters the NO_DEFAULT parameter. Also, if there is an EXIT command at the end of the system login script, no user script will run.

At login, how can I detect whether a workstation is using NETX or the VLMs?

VLMs report their NetWare version number in response to the SHELL_TYPE variable in a login script. For example, add the following lines to your system login script:

```
IF SHELL_TYPE  < "V4.00" THEN BEGIN
     FIRE PHASERS
     WRITE "It is time to upgrade your client software"
     PAUSE
     END
```

With this variable in place, NETX users will see the above message, but users of version 4.00 and higher will not. Each time the VLMs are upgraded, you can make the appropriate change to your IF statement.

How can I load a memory resident program (TSR) from my system login script?

Using the pound sign (#) before a DOS command in the login script will allow you to load a TSR. For example, to run a TSR called MYTSR, add the line **#MYTSR** in the login script.

Tech Terror: The system login script is executed by the LOGIN utility, which stays resident as long as the login script is running. Loading a TSR while the LOGIN utility is running can cause unpredictable results, so proceed with caution.

 ## Why do TSRs loaded from the login script take up so much memory?

When you use the pound sign (#) to load a TSR from a login script (see the preceding question), the TSR will take up a larger area of memory than normal. This occurs because the TSR is loaded in memory next to the temporary location of LOGIN. When the login script ends, LOGIN is removed from memory, but the TSR continues to occupy its own spot in memory as well as that of LOGIN. To avoid this problem, run TSRs from a batch file, after the EXIT command in the login script. Here is an example of a login script that accomplishes this, where *Start* is a batch file in the path:

```
EXIT "Start"
```

Keep in mind, also, that EXIT can also be used in conjunction with an IF statement in the login script, as shown in Figure 4-2.

```
SYSCON  3.62                                   Friday  March 4, 1994  4:32 pm
                    User SUPERVISOR On File Server GULAG-ARCH

                            System Login Script

MAP S11:=SYS:BMAIL\PROGRAM
IF "%DAY_OF_WEEK" = "WEDNESDAY" THEN EXIT "CSCAN"

Rem *** Special exit for various users
IF "%LOGIN_NAME" = "SUPERVISOR" THEN EXIT "START SYSTEM"
IF "%LOGIN_NAME" = "ADMIN" THEN EXIT "WPRINTER"
IF "%LOGIN_NAME" = "BUTCHER" THEN EXIT
IF "%LOGIN_NAME" = "ARCHIVER" THEN EXIT "TNAARC"
IF "%LOGIN_NAME" = "TNA" THEN EXIT "TNAARC1"
IF "%LOGIN_NAME" = "SERVICE" THEN EXIT
IF "%LOGIN_NAME" = "FACSYS" THEN EXIT

IF MEMBER OF "BMADMINS" THEN EXIT "BMADMIN"
IF MEMBER OF "WINDOWS" THEN EXIT "WSTART"

Rem EXIT FOR ALL OTHERS
EXIT "Start"
```

FIGURE 4-2   Using EXIT with IF in a login script

When I execute a menu from the DOS command line, it works, but when I try to execute the same menu from my user login script, it fails with an out-of-memory message. Why is this happening?

When a login script executes, it remains in conventional memory until all of the script's commands are completed. When you execute a menu command from a login script, you should do so by adding it to the end of an EXIT command at the end of the script, for example,

EXIT MENU *menuname*

If you don't call your menu in this manner, then it tries to run while the login script is still in memory. The EXIT command forces the login script to end, which in turn removes the login script from memory.

NetWare 4.*x*

How can I edit the system login script on a NetWare 4.*x* server?

Tech Tip: A good way to remember the order in which the Netware 4.*x* login scripts execute is to think of the acronym CPU: *c*ontainer/*p*rofile/*u*ser.

NetWare 4.*x* does not have a system login script. The closest equivalent is the *container login script*, which is sometimes called a system login script. However, the container script only applies to *users in a container*, not to *all users on a server*. In addition to the container login script, NetWare 4.*x* also uses a *profile login script* and a *user login script*.

Containers—part of the hierarchical naming scheme used with NDS—are typically geographical or organizational units. A user belongs to a specific container, such as SALES or NEWYORK. *Profiles* are more like groups—for instance, administrators or secretaries—and do not have boundaries. *Users*, of course, are still users in 4.*x*. After an upgrade to 4.*x*, the system login script remains on a server (in SYS:PUBLIC), and may still be accessed by users of bindery emulation (users who attach via NETX).

Are there any reported problems with NetWare 4.*x* login commands?

Yes. If you use the following syntax, the login script fails:

IF MEMBER OF *"groupname"*...

This failure occurs because of a bug in NetWare 4.*x*, and has been reported to Novell. Ironically, if you include the NOT operator on this line, as shown next, the login script will succeed with no errors.

IF NOT MEMBER OF *"groupname"*...

There is no workaround to this bug, other than creating groups specifically for the purpose of excluding their members.

Under NetWare 4.0, changes to a user login script do not appear immediately. Why?

Under NetWare 4.0—unlike NetWare 3.*x*—a user logs in to a network, not just to a server. The login for the network is controlled by NDS. Changes to the user login script are implemented by NDS and there may be a time lapse before they appear.

NetWare 3.*x*

How can I map a volume's subdirectory so that it appears as a root directory?

Use the MAP ROOT command. For example,

```
MAP ROOT G:= SERVER1/SYS:CORPORATE\APPS:
```

This command results in the APPS subdirectory appearing as G:\. Mapping through the Windows File Manager will result in a MAP ROOT, though you will see the entire path in the Windows title bar.

How can I use a login script to connect to more than one file server at a time?

Connect to other servers using the command syntax

ATTACH *servername\username*

You can connect to up to eight servers at once. This can be accomplished at the command line, through a login script, or through a batch file. In addition, mapping to a drive will cause NetWare to prompt you to attach to the server if you are not currently attached. The command WHOAMI tells you what servers you are attached to and what login name is used for each server. Figure 4-3 shows how the information is displayed.

Tech Tip: A semicolon (;) at the end of a string in a login script may not be recognized in older versions of LOGIN.EXE. This problem is corrected in version 3.65.

```
F:\PUBLIC>WHOAMI
You are user SUPERVISOR attached to server GULAG-ARCH, connection 1.
Server GULAG-ARCH is running NetWare v3.11 (250 user).
Login time: Friday  March  4, 1994  4:17 pm

You are user GUEST attached to server MOVIE-STAR, connection 1.
Server MOVIE-STAR is running NetWare v3.11 (250 user).
Login time: Friday  March  4, 1994  4:21 pm

You are user DGUARNIE attached to server DARK-HORSE, connection 1.
Server DARK-HORSE is running NetWare v3.11 (250 user).
Login time: Friday  March  4, 1994  4:23 pm
```

FIGURE 4-3   Sample output from the WHOAMI command

What does #COMMAND /C mean in my login script?

#COMMAND /C indicates that an internal DOS command will be executed. DOS commands such as CLS and DIR are internal to the COMMAND.COM file, and do not require a separate executable file. Refer to your DOS manual for a full listing of internal commands.

Tech Tip: This invocation—#Command /C—spawns a child command process. Versions of DOS before 3.30 used this to launch batch files from within batch files. You can now accomplish the same thing by using the CALL command.

Why do I see the error message, "Missing command name" when I run my system login script?

You have a pound sign (#) in your login script with no external DOS command following it. To fix this error, delete the # from your script or insert an external DOS command after the #.

I've just installed some machines running DOS 6 and NETX 3.26 on my network. When I try to boot them using my system login script, I get the error message, "Incorrect DOS version." What's wrong?

Machines installed with DOS 6 commonly come with DOS 5 for NETX hard-coded in SETVER. When NETX loads, DOS 6 emulates DOS 5 and causes the error message. One temporary solution is to remove SETVER from your CONFIG.SYS, or you can remove NETX from the SETVER table (SETVER NETX.EXE /D). However, if you have DOS 6, it's best to upgrade your NETX version to 3.32, as this version supports DOS 6 directly.

Tech Tip: With DOS 6, also look for problems in your directory structure. Configure your disk so that the OS version is in the format *x.xx;* for example, for version 6, the directory name should be 6.00. Also, look for misspellings in the system login script.

Why do I see the message, "Incorrect DOS version" when I exit from an application?

COMSPEC has probably been set incorrectly in the system login script. Either it is pointing to an incorrect version of DOS, or the COMMAND.COM that it's pointing to is corrupt. To fix the problem, either copy the correct version of COMMAND.COM into the correct path, or change the location where COMSPEC looks for COMMAND.COM.

To see where the current COMSPEC is set, use the DOS SET command. The system will return something like this:

```
PROMPT=$P$G
COMSPEC=X:COMMAND.COM
```

This setting must be accessible. If it points to the network, make sure that the COMMAND.COM located on the network drive is the exact same version as the one on the boot device.

How can I prevent user login scripts from executing after the system login script?

If a user has created a personal user login script, he or she may inadvertently alter some of the important systemwide assignments. To prevent this from happening, add the EXIT command at the end of your system login script. This command ends the system login script processing before it can check for a user login script. Keep in mind, however, that a user can still bypass the system login script by using the /S parameter at the end of the LOGIN command.

Tech Tip: Version 3.70 of LOGIN.EXE fixes some earlier-version problems. It contains an option to specify that no default login scripts are to be executed. It also lets you specify whether the workstation time should be synchronized with the file server. To receive LOGIN.EXE 3.70, download patch #1558 from Corporate Software's Electronic Services System bulletin board, or call their Product Support Hotline. A text file called LOG370.DOC comes with the patch and lists all the fixes made in 3.70.

How can I bypass the system login script?

It is possible to bypass the LOGIN procedure and gain access to the file server. This may be vital if there is something in the system login script that causes a fatal error, preventing anyone from logging in. You need to have a copy of the ATTACH and MAP command-line utilities in the \LOGIN directory or on your workstation. (You will find these command files on the original Public NetWare diskettes.) Load IPX and NETX; then, to make a connection to the server, use ATTACH with the following syntax:

ATTACH *fileservername*/*username*

Then map the server's public directory to a network drive, with the MAP command as follows:

MAP F:=*fileservername*\SYS:PUBLIC

Finally, run SYSCON from the network drive to correct the system login script.

With NetWare 386, it is also possible to direct LOGIN to run an alternate script file. For example, in these cases you might keep on your local drive an ASCII file that maps a network drive to the server volume. The syntax for executing the alternate login script is

LOGIN /S *path**script file* /N

Tech Tip: All login script commands and variables (such as DAY_OF_WEEK) must be in uppercase, or they may not be recognized by the program and will not execute properly.

Our network supervisor has set up a system login script that takes a long time to execute. Is there any way I can bypass it and just run my user login script?

Yes. Even though NetWare executes the system login script (if it exists) before a user login script, you can reverse this order by adding a special parameter to the end of the LOGIN command. Instead of simply typing LOGIN and pressing ENTER, you need to add /S and the complete path and filename of your user login script. For example, to log in to a server called SALES, your LOGIN command might look like this:

```
LOGIN /S SALES/SYS:MAIL\C000123\LOGIN
```

This example assumes that you are using NetWare's default storage location for user login scripts, which is your personal subdirectory in the MAIL directory. You can, however, use an ASCII text editor to create a login script and store it elsewhere. For example, suppose you created a login script called MYLOGIN.TXT and stored it in the PUBLIC directory of server SALES. Then your LOGIN command might look like this:

```
LOGIN /S SALES/SYS:PUBLIC\MYLOGIN.TXT
```

Logging in to a server in this way bypasses the system login script. Keep in mind, however, that some system login scripts execute important programs or display important system messages, and you will be excluded from these if you bypass the system login script. So use this method of logging in with caution. If you are unsure whether you should be using this method, check with your network administrator.

What does NetWare mean by the error message, "Invalid Command.Com"?

Make sure that you have the same version, size, and date on COMMAND.COM in the root directory of your boot drive and in the path that is referenced in the COMSPEC command. Also, COMMAND.COM could be missing. See also the question, "Why do I see the message, 'Incorrect DOS version' when I exit from an application?" earlier in this chapter.

Hosw can I use DOS variables in login scripts?

First make sure that the desired information is assigned to a DOS variable in the environment before

LOGIN executes. For example, COMSPEC = C:\COMMAND.COM establishes COMPSEC as an environmental variable. In the login script, you can reference the DOS variable in braces, for example,

```
IF <COMSPEC> = "C:\COMMAND.COM" THEN DOS SET
COMSPEC="S2:\COMMAND.COM"
```

We have a complicated startup procedure. How can I tell if the login to the network has been successful?

The NetWare LOGIN.EXE file returns an error level for use in batch files. It will return 0 if login is successful, or 1 if it fails. This error level can be trapped in a batch procedure and made to return a message to the user, indicating the status of the login.

Tech Tip: To copy a line from one login script to another, highlight the line you want to copy by using the F5 key and the arrow keys. Delete the text, paste it back at the same location, and then open another login script and insert the line (the text block stays in the buffer).

NetWare Directory Services

In NetWare 4.*x*, NetWare Directory Services (NDS)
replaces the bindery found in versions 3.*x* and earlier.
The bindery was a flat ASCII file, but NDS puts the
power of a full relational database in the hands of the
administrator. Just as importantly, NDS is an
enterprise—wide system, in contrast to the server-based
concepts and constructions in earlier versions of
NetWare. NDS also replaces the text screen found in the
earlier NetWare utilities with a full Windows interface.

For what it's worth, Novell claims that NDS follows
the ISO x.500 standard for directory services. It
introduces a hierarchical tree of objects as the
organizational structure for the entire network. All
network resources are considered objects. (Previously
there was an elemental distinction between certain
types of objects; servers and users, for example, were
not a part of the same hierarchy.) Now each object in
the NDS tree can have a sophisticated list of properties,
which are free of associations with any specific physical
resource such as a server. The NDS tree also provides for
multiple organizational levels, as well as common names
for all objects.

FRUSTRATION BUSTERS!

- Keep the NDS tree simple to start with. Don't nest to a level of complexity that becomes cumbersome.

- Make sure you develop the habit of backing up NDS regularly.

- For fast on-line help, learn to use the CX utility.

- Use the Partition Manager utility to maintain and administer the NDS database files.

What guidelines should I follow for implementing naming standards for NDS?

Create an NDS naming-standards document that details the order, types of abbreviations, and property values for all directory objects. When possible, base the tree on the operational structure of the organization that the network is serving. Keep the tree as simple as possible, and plan for future additions. For example, build the organization beneath the root, and then put the location organization units beneath the organization. Each location organization can include container objects such as users, groups, servers, profiles, and services. This type of structure is extremely scaleable.

Plan the tree from the top down, and move down the tree one level at a time when you're planning. Too many levels can lead to performance and administration problems. Make the setting of contexts as simple as possible. For example, a given location organizational unit might include a statement such as the following in its profile login script:

```
CONTEXT OU.=BLD1.0=GM
```

This statement allows users to enter just a login name and password when they log in, instead of having to set a context.

Finally, plan for well-distributed repetition of partitions. Base partition repetition on logical boundaries, and then replicate partitions where you wish to decrease traffic.

What is an inherited right?

In the global directory, object and property rights flow from the top of the structure down the tree. When rights flow down the tree, they are known as *inherited rights.* The rights you actually have to a directory or file are *effective rights.*

How can I back up NDS?

NDS is a relational database, and the files are always open—they cannot be backed up by simple copy commands. In order to reliably back up NDS, you must use a backup application that is compliant with Novell's Storage Management System (SMS), such as SBACKUP, an NLM that ships with NetWare 4.*x.* To back up NDS, load SBACKUP.NLM and TSA_NDS.NLM at the file server console, and then select Backup Directory Services.

Tech Tip: SBACKUP is a very basic backup utility that is provided free with NetWare 4.*x.* If you are interested in more full-featured backup programs, many third-party SMS-compliant alternatives to SBACKUP are currently under development, at vendors such as Cheyenne and Emerald.

Tech Tip: Directory Information Base (DIB) is the actual database file that is maintained by NDS. The DIB is distributed and replicated across the servers in a NetWare 4.0 directory tree.

What is bindery emulation?

NDS can emulate the flat structure of the NetWare 2.*x*/3.*x* bindery. This *bindery emulation* feature allows clients to log in using NETX. When bindery emulation is on, bindery-based clients and utilities will see all leaf objects in the server's bindery context as if they were in a bindery. This limits the effectiveness of NDS, but allows users who are not 4.0 clients to log in and use the network.

What is a NetWare server object?

Bindery-based servers (2.*x*/3.*x*) can be added to the 4.*x* directory tree as NetWare server objects. This lets NDS users access volumes on those servers just as they can NetWare 4.*x* volumes. Use NETADMIN or NWADMIN to create NetWare server and volume objects for the server you are adding to the tree, as shown here:

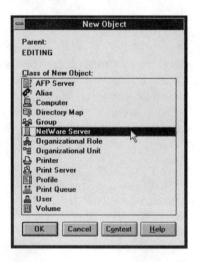

This is the flip side of the question just above. Users of the 4.*x* client software will have access to 3.*x* servers. Both of these situations are important during the transition period for networks moving to Netware 4.*x* and VLM technology.

Can I have two server objects with the same name on an NDS enterprise network?

No. This is a limitation of SAP rather than NDS. Make sure that every object on the enterprise network has a unique name.

How does auto-tuning work?

NetWare 4.*x* performs several auto-tuning functions that automatically adjust NetWare's configuration for changes in the production workload. These functions are

- Service processes
- Directory caching
- Physical packet receive buffers

In every case, auto-tuning increases the number of resources available to the operating system. These increases occur when there is an available resource. When the server detects a need for additional bandwidth in any of the auto-tuning parameters, the parameter is increased. You can also limit auto-tuning by using the SET command to set lower limits for the auto-tuned parameters.

What is an Access Control List?

All objects can have a property known as the *Access Control List (ACL)*, which controls access to the object as well as its properties. For both the object and its properties, the ACL lists who has rights (trustees) and what those rights are (rights assignments).

How do I remove NDS from a NetWare 4.x file server?

Use the following procedure to remove NDS from a NetWare 4.*x* file server. Do not delete the server object from NDS or remove the physical server from the network without first completing these steps.

1. Run PARTMGR (Partition Manager) to remove all replicas from the file server—unless the server holds a master replica of a given partition. If it holds a master replica, you must assign a new master replica on a different server.

2. Load INSTALL.NLM, and select Maintenance Selective Install, then Directory Options, followed by Remove Directory Services from this Server.

3. Log in to NDS with Supervisor rights. Using NETADMIN, delete this server's volume objects, which will now appear as Unknown objects.

What is a Reference Time Server?

A Reference Time Server (RTS) provides a time to which all other servers and clients synchronize, and is used when it is important to have a central point to control network time. Reference Time Servers should be synchronized with an accurate external time source, such as a radio clock that receives time signals from the U.S. Naval Observatory. An RTS polls other RTSs or Primary Time Servers (PTSs), and then votes with them to synchronize the time. Because the RTS does not change its clock, the PTSs must reach consensus with the time provided by the RTS.

What is a Primary Time Server?

A Primary Time Server (PTS) synchronizes network time with at least one other PTS or RTS, and provides the time to Secondary Time Servers (STSs) and clients. A PTS polls other PTSs or RTSs, and then votes with them to synchronize the time. PTSs adjust their internal clocks to synchronize with the agreed common network time. Because all PTSs adjust their clocks, network time may drift slightly during this process. A PTS is used primarily on larger networks, to increase fault tolerance by providing redundant paths for STSs. If a PTS goes down, an STS can get the time from an alternate PTS. On a large network, use at least one PTS for every 125 to 150 STSs.

What is a Single Reference Time Server?

A Single Reference Time Server (SRTS) provides time to STSs and clients. When an SRTS is used, it is the sole source of time for the entire network. The network supervisor sets the time on the SRTS, which is the default time server installed with NetWare 4.*x*. SRTS is recommended for use primarily with small networks.

What is a Secondary Time Server?

A *Secondary Time Server (STS)* obtains the time from a Single Reference, Primary, or Reference Time Server. The STS provides the time to clients, such as workstations and applications. An STS does not vote to determine the correct network time. If you have designated a server on the network as an SRTS, you must designate all other servers on the network as STSs. If you have designated several servers on the network as PTSs or RTSs, then designate all other servers on the network as STSs. To keep network traffic between the time servers to a minimum, have STSs contact PTSs or RTSs that are physically close. For optimal time synchronization, require each STS to contact a PTS, RTS, or SRTS with as few intervening routers and slow LAN segments as possible.

Client/Requester Installation and Maintenance

Clients are the primary interface through which users receive information on the network; they are the software link between the workstation and the network operating system. Novell supports an ever-expanding universe of client platforms. In this chapter, we've gathered questions and answers about DOS, OS/2, and Macintosh clients.

Beginning with NetWare 4.0, Novell refers to the DOS client software portion of NetWare as the NetWare DOS *Requester*. For DOS and OS/2 clients, NetWare supports four protocols: native IPX/SPX, Named Pipes, TCP/IP, and NetBIOS. For the Macintosh client, NetWare supports AFP. Further, within DOS there are three choices for workstation configuration: the original IPX created with WSGEN (the monolithic drivers), the ODI drivers that are used in any multiprotocol environment, and the new NetWare VLMs. Ironically, VLMs are instrumental in supporting the introduction of network peer-based services such as Personal NetWare, and this begins to blur the distinction between client and server, or at the very least, makes the client and server archetypes much more complex. UnixWare, Windows NT, and the IPX stack for the Mac will add further complexity to the client issue in the not-too-distant future.

FRUSTRATION BUSTERS!

- When you're troubleshooting a workstation, don't overlook the obvious: check the cable. Loose connections, bad cards, and faulty cables are still the most prevalent causes of workstation problems.

- As much as possible, minimize the number of different types of adapter cards used on the network. NICs that are 100% interchangeable are easy to replace and need not be reconfigured.

- Minimize the amount of software loaded at the workstation—let the network do the job it's meant to do; the software will be easier to manage from a central location.

- To facilitate troubleshooting, keep copies of the standard configuration files—AUTOEXEC.BAT, CONFIG.SYS, SHELL.CFG, and NET.CFG—on a diskette or server.

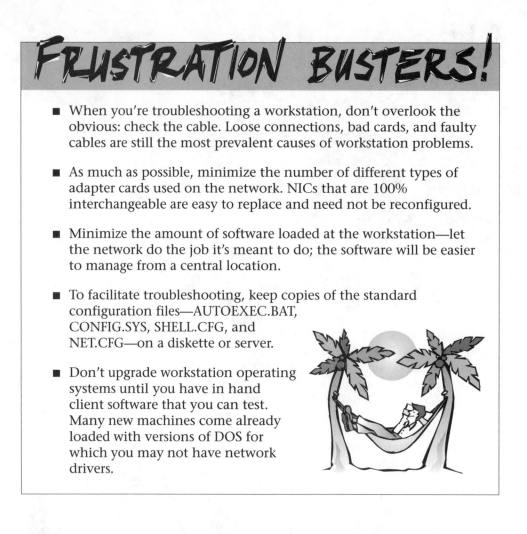

- Don't upgrade workstation operating systems until you have in hand client software that you can test. Many new machines come already loaded with versions of DOS for which you may not have network drivers.

What version of NETX do I need to use with DOS 6.x?

For DOS 6.x versions (6.0, 6.1, and 6.2), use NETX version 3.32 or higher, which is available on CompuServe in the NOVLIB forum as NET33X.EXE. Or use the NetWare VLM Client 1.x; this comes with NetWare 3.12 or 4.x.

How can I determine which version of the NetWare shell is running?

Type NVER and the version of the shell will be displayed on the screen.

How can I run the NetWare shell in expanded or extended memory?

Follow these steps:

Tech Tip: If you are using DOS 5 or higher, it is possible to load the standard NETX into high memory with the LH command.

1. Locate HIMEM.SYS and EMM386.EXE on your hard drive (they're probably in the DOS directory). Use a word processor or text editor to modify CONFIG.SYS, and add the following lines, substituting the variable *pathname* with the actual pathname of the files on your system:

    DEVICE=C:*pathname*\\HIMEM.SYS
    DEVICE=C:*pathname*\\EMM386.EXE RAM

2. Copy XMSNETX.EXE (extended memory) or EMSNETX.EXE (expanded memory) from the WSGEN diskette to the directory where the NetWare workstation files are located.

3. Modify AUTOEXEC.BAT (and any other relevant batch files) to use XMSNETX.EXE or EMSNETX.EXE as the NetWare shell, instead of NETX.COM.

4. Finally, load the new drivers by rebooting the PC.

How can I force a workstation to log in to a specific server?

One way is to edit or create a NET.CFG or SHELL.CFG file that contains the following statement:

preferred server=*fileservername*

Alternatively, you can add the following parameter to the NETX or VLM command:

/ps=*fileservername*

The foregoing method, however, only sets the user default server and does not force login to a specific server.

When I attempt to run NETX, why do I get the message, "A File Server could not be found"?

This message is generated by the shell when trying to build a connection with the network. It means no file server responded to the request, and NETX timed out. Either the station is not on the network, the network drivers are incorrect, or the server is not running. This could be caused by a loose or malfunctioning cable, a defective network interface card, an incorrect IPX configuration, or a file server going down. Check the cable, and run IPX /I to determine if the shell configuration matches the settings for the NIC in use at that workstation.

There are also several other causes for this condition that are specific to 4.0. See the relevant question regarding the same error message in the 4.*x* section of this chapter.

What does NetWare mean by the message, "Network Device Fault Reading Drive"?

This may occur while you are in an application, even if you haven't touched the keyboard for a while. The error appears to be generated by the application but points to the network as the problem. This message tells you there is some sort of communications problem between the workstation and the server. Look for problems with the connectivity between the workstation and the server (check the NIC, the cabling, any bridges or routers, and so forth). Most likely, you will have to reboot.

I just got the message, "You are not connected to any file servers. The shell will try to connect to a file server whenever the current default drive is changed to a valid drive." What does NetWare mean?

Your current drive is a network drive, and the shell has lost its connection to the network. This could be the result of downed file servers or problems with the infrastructure—cables, hubs, routers and so on. Change your directory to a local drive, and then change back to a network drive. The shell will automatically attempt to reattach to the first available server. If that doesn't do the trick, reboot. TSRs may have been loaded, or parts of the environment may be corrupt or unable to reattach.

What does NetWare mean by the message, "File server *servername* cannot support any more connections"?

This occurs during login, and tells you that the maximum amount of users allowed under your current NetWare server license are already logged in to your server. (Remember that print servers and some NLM processes take connections, too.) You must wait until a connection becomes available. It may be time to consider upgrading your server license to accommodate more users.

What does NetWare mean by the message, "Volume *x* is almost out of disk space"?

This message at the bottom of the workstation screen indicates that your server's disk space is very low and needs attention. You should delete old or unwanted files immediately. Consider adding new volumes to your server (or talk to your administrator about it). You can start by purging any deleted files that are still on the hard drive. Purged files are deleted based on a timer in NetWare—not on users' disk space requirements.

When I try to use the SEND utility, I get the message, "Message NOT sent to *servername/username*." What's wrong?

One of several issues could be responsible for the problem. Is the *username* valid? Is that user logged in to the network? If either of these conditions is not met, your message will fail. Has the receiving user disabled messages with the CASTOFF command? In this case, no messages will be received successfully. Tell this user to use CASTON to enable messages.

If you've sent several messages to this user already, the pipeline may be "clogged." The SEND utility will only buffer two messages at a time. If your first message is still displayed on the receiving workstation (the user has not yet cleared it with CTRL-ENTER), that means your second message is in the buffer, so the user's workstation cannot accept any more messages until the first message on the screen is cleared.

Since upgrading to VLMs, I receive this error message whenever I print: "Windows Cannot Write to this File. Disk May be Full." I increased the FILEHANDLES parameter in NET.CFG, but the problem persists. Why?

With VLMs, the FILEHANDLES statement in NET.CFG is no longer valid. To solve the problem, increase the FILES statement in CONFIG.SYS. When running Windows, this setting should be FILES=100 or more.

Tech Tip: If you're running Windows, be sure to create swap files on local disks instead of the network, or you may find the network grinding to a halt.

Which IRQs should *not* be used with an IBM 16/4 Token Ring adapter running the NetWare Requester for OS/2?

The Requester uses IRQ 9 to communicate. If the IRQ for the adapter card is set to either 2 or 9, there will be an IRQ conflict.

Tech Tip: If you need to use IRQ2, or an IRQ that is considered in use by the peripheral interrupt controller (PIC), then you need to install Novell patch VPICDA.386. If a message persists after installing this patch, use another IRQ for your network card. Good interrupts to consider are IRQ 3 (which is COM2) or, if you have a 386 or 486 machine, a 16-bit interrupt such as 10. ODI drivers set these parameters in the NET.CFG file; the monolithic drivers set these options when running WSGEN.

Why does a NIC's I/O base address of 360H conflict with LPT1 when LPT1's I/O base address is 378H-37FH?

NICs generally use an address range of 20H I/O. This means the range of the base address 360H would be 360H to 37FH. Since LPT1's I/O base address 378H-37FH falls within that range, a conflict results.

I am running NetBIOS to communicate with my Lotus Notes server. Other users in my department report adequate response time, but mine is terrible. What's wrong?

NetBIOS under NetWare is timing sensitive, and to adjust your NetBIOS communications dialog with the Notes server, you need to tune several parameters in your NET.CFG. Adjusting these parameters can result in significant performance improvements—but it also requires memory. Though the default value for the NetBIOS command is 12, the range is 4 to 250; the higher the number, the better. And though the default for both the NetBIOS receive and send buffers is 6, the range is 4 to 20. Check to see if these parameters are set differently on your station than on the stations experiencing better performance.

What should I do when a Token Ring workstation can't find the file server?

First, do some commonsense troubleshooting. Make sure the cable is properly connected to both the MAU port and the Token Ring NIC. At the MAU end, the connector will click when you connect it to the port. Next, use a diagnostic utility to make sure the Token Ring NIC is functioning properly (most NICs include a diagnostic utility). As with most troubleshooting procedures, swapping parts often helps identify faulty ones. Try swapping the cable, the NIC, and even the workstation to see what solves the problem.

I am running NetBIOS to communicate with my Lotus Notes server, but I periodically lose my connection and see an error message that the Notes server is not responding. Re-accessing the server right away only works about half the time—even though the server seems okay. What's the problem?

NetBIOS is sensitive to timing delays, and these can be introduced by *internetwork links* (think of them as *segment hops*). If your Notes server is on the backbone, the hops across segments introduce timing delays that cause the NetBIOS connection to time out. There are a number of parameters you can set in the NET.CFG file to tune the timing between devices communicating via NetBIOS. Check the System Administration manual, and adjust your NetBIOS parameters to fit your environment. For example, you can increase the NetBIOS Retry Count and the NetBIOS Retry Delay in either NET.CFG or SHELL.CFG.

What is burst mode?

Burst mode is a method for stringing multiple NetWare packets together so that the file server only sends a single acknowledgment packet for the entire group, rather than for each individual packet. This typically improves performance for many applications, especially the ones that load large files. By default, NetWare 4.*x* and NetWare 3.12 have burst mode active; NetWare 3.*x* requires a separate set of NLMs to enable burst mode. Installation of burst mode requires changes on both the client and the file server.

Can burst mode improve performance?

Burst mode helps improve performance by allowing NetWare clients to send several packets to the server before requiring a response. By default, the client must receive a response to each packet it sends. BNETX, which is burst mode in versions prior to 3.12, is no longer available on

NetWire, but burst mode is built into the VLMs and the NetWare 4.0 and 3.12 operating systems. For NetWare 3.12, run PBURST.NLM from the Client Kit. A client workstation can run under the VLMs contained in the Client Kit.

If there are multiple NETX statements in my AUTOEXEC.BAT file, does my workstation load NETX more than once? Does this affect the conventional memory in my workstation?

Your workstation will only load NETX once, no matter how many times the command appears in your AUTOEXEC.BAT file. After the first load, NetWare will return the following error message if it encounters another NETX statement:

```
NetWare Workstation Shell has already been loaded.
```

Under certain circumstances, NETX can be safely loaded into high memory, depending on your PC architecture and the version of DOS you're using. Under DOS 5 and above, this is accomplished through LOADHIGH.

Tech Terror: Be careful when using LOADHIGH, and make sure you take into account the requirements of all the applications you're running. LOADHIGH can affect performance negatively, and some TSRs cannot be unloaded.

What does NetWare mean by the message, "Error Receiving from Network, Abort Retry Ignore"?

The workstation has timed out while waiting for a response from the file server. This can be caused by hardware problems, by high-traffic situations, or by a temporarily overworked file server. Try increasing the IPX Retry Count in SHELL.CFG to 60. Although this may cause the response to be slow, the shell triples the number of attempts to retry its requests before timing out, and the additional retry attempts may allow the server sufficient time to respond.

Why does NETX indicate that I'm running DOS 5 when I'm running DOS 6?

On most PCs, SETVER.EXE is automatically loaded in CONFIG.SYS. This allows you to specify an older version of DOS for a particular program. In the SETVER table, NETX is defined to require DOS 5. Therefore, when NETX attempts to load, SETVER tells NETX it is running under DOS 5 and thus causes the error. One solution is to not load SETVER.EXE (remove the line from your CONFIG.SYS). Or you can update the SETVER table to reflect the correct version of DOS, by typing the following at the command line:

```
SETVER NETX.EXE 6.00
```

For NETX to report the correct DOS version, you must be using NETX 3.32. NETX 3.26 will operate, but will not return the proper DOS environment parameter if you try to identify the OS version through NetWare.

The commands in my NET.CFG produce an error, even though their syntax appears to be correct. What's wrong?

Entries in NET.CFG must be typed in a specific format. Options must be flush left, one per line; and settings must be indented under their option, one setting per line. For example:

```
Link Driver 3C503
  frame = ethernet_802.3
```

Also, there should be a hard return (CR/LF) after each line, including the last line.

Why does my machine hang when I run IPX?

There may be multiple IPX.COM files specified in your path, or there is an interrupt conflict with the NIC.

NetWare 4.x

When I attempt to log in to a NetWare 4.x file server, I get this message: "Your current context is *xxxxx.xxxxx*. The user specified does not exist in this context. Login will try to find the user in the server context." What's wrong?

This message appears when LOGIN cannot find your username in the current context or bindery context. To resolve the problem, specify the full name of the user when logging in, for example:

LOGIN *servername* /CN=*xxxx*.O=*xxxx*

You can also specify the default context in the NET.CFG file. To do so, add the following line to the NetWare DOS Requester section of NET.CFG:

NAME CONTEXT="OU=*xxxx*.OU=*xxxx*.O=*xxxx*"

There is also a command called CX that displays the current context. Using CX in conjunction with other parameters allows you to change the current context.

Tech Tip: In the commands specified just above, CN is the Common Name (user name), O is Organization, and OU is the Organization Unit. The periods are qualifiers. The naming tree is hierarchical, so you can have multiple organizational units.

What is the DOS Requester and how does it work?

The NetWare DOS Requester, introduced with NetWare 4.0, is the DOS client software portion of NetWare. It is a group of separate modules that performs the tasks of NETX.COM and adds other features as well. The DOS Requester runs with DOS 3.1 and higher.

VLM.EXE is the first DOS Requester module loaded; it manages the memory utilization of other Requester modules. VLM.EXE includes a list of default Virtual Loadable Modules (VLMs), and others can be added. The Requester offers services in the following three areas:

- DOS Redirection Layer
- Service Protocol Layer
- Transport Protocol Layer

After running the installation program for the NetWare DOS Requester, I receive this error message when loading Windows: "The NetWare VLM is not loaded or is not configured correctly." What's wrong?

This often occurs when you're using NETX as the shell, instead of the VLMs. If you installed Windows support when installing the VLMs, you cannot use NETX anymore. You must use the VLMs.

When I attempt to attach to a NetWare 4.x file server, I see the message, "File Server Could Not Be Found." What are some of the possible causes?

There are several possible causes that are specific to NetWare 4.*x*. (Numerous other causes that are not version specific are usually hardware related. For more information, see the relevant question about this message earlier in this chapter.)

One cause is using Ethernet 802.3 on the client, because the latest versions of the MLID drivers (such as NE2000.COM) default to the Ethernet 802.2 frame type. In the Link Driver section of the NET.CFG, change the frame type to Ethernet 802.3. If *both* the Ethernet 802.2 and

Ethernet 802.3 frame types are defined in the Link Driver section of the NET.CFG, make sure that Ethernet 802.3 appears *first*.

Also, if you quit INSTALL before installing NetWare Directory Services (NDS), the server will not advertise itself, and so you cannot attach or log in to the network. To determine if NDS is installed, use the following procedure:

1. From the file server console, load INSTALL.NLM.

2. From the main menu, select Maintenance/Selective Install.

3. From the Maintenance menu, select Directory Options.

4. Select Install Directory Services Onto This Server.

If Directory Services is already installed, the following message will be displayed:

```
This server already contains Directory Services Information
```

If you do not receive this message, it means NDS is not installed, and you may continue to install it. When there is only one NetWare 4.0 server, type **DISPLAY SERVERS** at the command line and look for the server name and directory tree name. They will not appear if NDS is not installed.

 My Lotus Notes server keeps displaying a "TRAP D" error message. What does this relate to?

You are probably using the NetBIOS driver with the NetWare OS/2 2.01 Requester that Novell shipped with NetWare 4.0. If so, you must download the latest NETBIOS.SYS file from NetWire, or call Novell to obtain the latest version. This will allow you to run Notes Release 3 over NetBIOS protocol with OS/2 version 2.1. You'll thus resolve problems with the workstation trapping, allow 255 sessions, and close resources correctly when the application terminates. Replace the NETBIOS.SYS file in the directory that stores the NetWare for OS/2 drivers, and reboot OS/2. Further instructions on how to install NETBIOS.SYS are in the OS2V2A.TXT file within OS2V2A.EXE (the download file from NetWire).

Tech Terror: The patch in OS2V2A is provided as is, and is covered by Novell under their unverified patch disclaimer. Make sure you are backed up before attempting to install or use it! Also, be sure you are using a network adapter that is supported by the 2.01 release and is one that Lotus claims will work.

Why would I use Signature Level=1?

Setting the Signature Level in NET.CFG allows for *NCP packet signature,* which is a message digest (similar to a checksum) that prevents unauthorized access to the network via forged packets. The first several bytes in a request packet go through a digest algorithm. The possible Signature Level settings are 0 for disabled, 1 for enabled but not preferred, 2 for preferred, and 3 for required.

If set to anything other than 0 or 1, this entry can impede performance; however, this slight decrease in performance must be weighed against the security benefits offered by NCP packet signing.

NetWare 3.*x*

What does NetWare mean by the message, "IPX has not been loaded. Please load and then run the shell"?

This occurs when loading NETX and indicates that you are attempting to load NETX before loading IPX. In order for NETX to redirect commands to your network, IPX must be loaded first.

What versions of IPX and NETX should I be using with Windows 3.1?

With Windows 3.1, use

- IPX 3.10 or higher
- NETX 3.26 or higher, or 3.32 for DOS 6.*x*

I attach to the network by loading IPX and NETX. Why does NetWare display the error message "Not ready error reading drive F:" when I try to log in?

Look in CONFIG.SYS for a RAMDrive. RAMDrives can interfere with the way LOGIN.EXE is trying to set up network drives. Refer to the RAMDrive documentation to see if there are special parameters required for loading in a network configuration.

I have an IPX.COM that matches my network card but doesn't match the card's configuration. What can I do?

You must regenerate IPX.

1. Insert the NetWare WSGEN diskette in one of the floppy drives.

2. At the command line, type **JUMPERS** *D:*, where *D:* is the drive that contains the WSGEN diskette.

3. The program will prompt for the name and location of the IPX.COM you want to modify. Provide a path and filename, and choose a new network card configuration.

4. Save the settings and exit.

Tech Tip: The WSGEN diskette is only available with NetWare 3.11 and below. In later releases of NetWare, it is assumed you will be using the ODI drivers. VLMs (and thus ODI drivers) are required for NetWare 4.*x*, but you can still use IPX.COM and NETX to access a NetWare 3.12 server.

I just copied the new client shell into my workstation's Novell directory. Why is the old NetWare shell executing when I run NETX?

The new NetWare workstation shell is NETX.EXE. The old shell is NETX.COM. DOS executes .COM files before .EXE files. Delete the old NETX.COM file and try again.

I am running NetBIOS on my workstation, and have parameters set in NET.CFG for tuning NetBIOS, but they don't seem to be taking effect. What's wrong?

NETBIOS.EXE will find and execute NET.CFG if both are in the same directory; otherwise, NET.CFG is ignored. Move the NETBIOS.EXE into the directory that stores your NET.CFG file, and this will solve the problem. You do not have to be logged in to the directory where the files reside, as long as they are in the path.

What are SHELL.CFG and NET.CFG, and how are they different?

Both SHELL.CFG and NET.CFG set parameters for a workstation when it boots, including how the workstation handles packets, print jobs, DOS versions, and search drives. You don't need to run both files, although it is permissible to do so. SHELL.CFG is a subset of NET.CFG, so standard procedure is to consolidate the two by copying SHELL.CFG into NET.CFG. The major difference between the two files is that NET.CFG allows the use of protocols in addition to IPX, whereas SHELL.CFG deals with IPX workstations only.

Tech Tip: Make sure that only one NET.CFG file and one SHELL.CFG file exist on the boot device. Regardless of your path setting, NetWare uses the .CFG file that's in the directory from which you run IPX, not necessarily the one in the directory that contains the IPX file.

How do I implement burst mode on a NetWare 3.11 server?

To implement burst mode, run PBURST.NLM on the file server and install BNETX.COM at the workstation. Burst mode buffers must also be configured in the client's NET.CFG. The resulting increase in performance can be anywhere from 10% to 300%, depending on the network environment. Networks that process a large number of file transactions, or networks that use many bridges and routers would benefit from using burst mode. Both the client and the server must be running the appropriate burst mode programs.

What version of the ODI drivers do I need in order to run Windows 3.x?

Following are the appropriate ODI driver versions for Windows 3.x:

Driver	Version	Command-Line Verification
NETX	3.26 or higher, or 3.32 for DOS 6.x	NETX I
IPXODI	1.20 or higher	IPXODI
TBMI2.COM	2.1 or higher	TBMI2
LSL.COM	1.21 or higher	LSL

Tech Tip: When installing Windows on a network, if users frequently move from one workstation to another, configure Windows with a temporary swap file. Otherwise, Windows will find the swap file corrupt each time a user logs in at a new location.

What does NetWare mean by the error message, "Different <IPX or LSL> or a <IPX or LSL> interrupt has been hooked"?

This means you tried to unload the IPX or LSL file from memory, but the file detected a condition that would not allow it to be removed safely. Either the resident IPXODI or LSL and the one used to unload the resident file are not the same version, or another program has been loaded that has hooked one of IPXODI's or LSL's interrupt vectors. They use the following interrupt vectors:

IPXODI	LSL
INT 08h	INT 08h
INT 2Fh	INT 2Fh
INT 64h	
INT 7Ah	

To fix this problem, try using the same versions of IPXODI or LSL for load and unload. If that doesn't work, unload the program that has hooked to one or more IPX or LSL interrupt vectors, and then unload IPXODI or LSL.

What does NetWare mean by the message, "FATAL: This old LSL is not supported"?

LSL is used by the ODI workstation drivers. The version of LSL.COM that you are using is out of date. Obtain a new one from NetWire.

What does NetWare mean by the message, "FATAL: There is a TSR above the loaded LSL"?

You are attempting to unload LSL.COM when there is another TSR program loaded after it. For LSL.COM to be successfully unloaded, you must first unload the TSR that was loaded after LSL.COM. To determine which file this is, type **MEM/C I MORE** at the command line. This will show the files in memory (MORE is used to prevent the screen from scrolling). Figure 6-1 shows a sample of the results of this command.

```
Conventional Memory :

Name              Size in Decimal      Size in Hex
-------------     ---------------      -----------
IBMDOS            17072   ( 16.7K)        42B0
HIMEM              4304   (  4.2K)        10D0
STACKER           45008   ( 44.0K)        AFD0
COMMAND            2624   (  2.6K)        A40
SHARE             17888   ( 17.5K)        45E0
SNAP             105872   (103.4K)        19D90
MOUSE             15328   ( 15.0K)        3BE0
LSL                3792   (  3.7K)        ED0
3C507              4640   (  4.5K)        1220
IPXODI            15888   ( 15.5K)        3E10
NETX              43728   ( 42.7K)        AAD0
FREE                 64   (  0.1K)        40
FREE                 64   (  0.1K)        40
FREE             377712   (368.9K)        5C370

Total   FREE :   377840      (369.0K)

Total bytes available to programs :        377840   (369.0K)
Largest executable program size :          377568   (368.7K)
-- More --
```

FIGURE 6-1   Sample memory output to the console

Why does WSGEN look for a disk in one of the floppy drives?

If you are trying to run WSGEN from a network drive or a local hard drive and the directory structure is not set up correctly, WSGEN will look for the A and B floppy drives and get caught in an endless loop. Novell knows about this bug and is working on a solution. The workaround is to use the directory structure on the hard drive, as depicted here:

```
├─NETWARE
     └─WSGEN
          WSGEN.EXE
```

All files from the WSGEN directory LAN_DRV_.001 are required (all LAN driver files). However, if you are running NetWare 3.11 or greater, now is the time to switch to the ODI drivers.

Why does the value for LONG MACHINE TYPE appear as IBM_PC, no matter what I put in SHELL.CFG?

When using the LONG MACHINE TYPE parameter in SHELL.CFG, you must use either four or six character values, or SHELL.CFG will use the default value (IBM_PC). In addition, if you use the SHORT MACHINE TYPE parameter in SHELL.CFG, you must use either three or four characters, or SHELL.CFG will use the default value (IBM).

Tech Tip: The SHORT MACHINE TYPE parameter is mostly used to map the correct version of DOS. Compaqs are set to SHORT MACHINE TYPE=CMPQ, and so on.

What does NetWare mean by the message, "Windows cannot write to this file. The disk may be full. Delete any unwanted files and then try again"?

This error may occur when you upgrade to VLMs, if the FILES parameter in CONFIG.SYS is not set high enough to accommodate the new environment. The error tells you that Windows is running out of file handles for creating temporary files. To solve the problem, increase the FILES statement in CONFIG.SYS to 100. If you are running many applications at once, 100 is not unreasonable, since each application can have 10 or more files open.

Prior to the introduction of VLM, FILES was typically set low in CONFIG.SYS and high in the NET.CFG file. However, the FILE HANDLES parameter is no longer valid with VLMs, so a higher FILES statement is required in CONFIG.SYS.

Why doesn't SET WORKSTATION TIME work properly?

The SET WORKSTATION TIME=OFF setting doesn't work properly unless you are running shell version 3.31 or higher.

How can I synchronize my workstation time with my file server time?

SYSTIME will synchronize your workstation time to the time of a specified file server. At the command line, type

    SYSTIME servername

SYSTIME is useful in the system login script, to set the time automatically on the workstation whenever a user logs in.

What does NetWare mean by the error message, "No Free NCBs"?

If you receive this message and the workstation hangs, try editing SHELL.CFG and increasing the NetBIOS sessions from the default of 32 to 100. Insert the following line in the file:

```
NetBIOS SESSION=100
```

If the SHELL.CFG file does not exist, you are using the default values, and you'll need to create the file.

What does NetWare mean by the message, "Error unloading NetWare shell—Different NetWare shell or a NetWare shell interrupt has been hooked"?

This occurs when you're trying to unload the NETX.COM shell when another shell component, such as NETBIOS.EXE, has been loaded. This error also may appear if you have another application or TSR that uses NetWare shell interrupts, or if a memory manager has moved the NETX.COM shell into high memory. To unload the NETX.COM shell, first remove all TSRs and applications that use NetWare shell interrupts. You cannot unload the shell if it has been loaded high with a memory manager.

When I try to load NETX at the command line, the shell starts to load, displays the message "Running," and then hangs my workstation. What's wrong?

The machine is probably not hung. When you try to load NETX, the shell looks for a server with which to connect. If for some reason the connection is bad, it will take a few minutes before returning the following error:

```
A File Server Could Not Be Found
```

My old network card died and I replaced it with a different type. Why does my workstation lock up when I try to log in?

You need to run WSGEN and regenerate IPX.COM to fit the specifications of your new card. IPX is specific to the base I/O and memory settings on your card. You probably have inserted a card with settings that are not similar to those of the old card; hence, IPX will not run. If you are using ODI drivers, you can modify NET.CFG to correct the settings. Typically, the information you need is as follows:

INT *interrupt #*
PORT *I/O port address* (in hex)
DMA *direct memory access channel* (usually 1, 2, or 3)
MEM *shared memory address* (in hex)
SLOT *number specifying slot number for EISA or MC machines*

Macintosh

With a 100-user version of NetWare and a 200-user version of NetWare for the Macintosh, how many Macs can connect at the same time?

You are limited by the number of NetWare server connections. In this case, only 100 Macs could connect at one time.

If I upgrade my NetWare 3.11 server to NetWare 3.12, do I need to upgrade my NetWare for Macintosh 3.011 as well?

Yes.

What causes different zones to appear each time I open up Chooser on my Macintosh?

Check your AppleTalk routers. All routers on the same network segment must share the same zone list and network address.

Zone lists that do not match can cause zones to appear and disappear from the Chooser. Slow links and/or intermittent connections can create this problem. Mixing NetWare and Apple routers in parallel can also cause differences in the router table. On a large network, it may take time for all the devices to report.

After I restore files to my Mac volume, the files appear but are unavailable. What's wrong?

Mac users may not have rights to the files, and if so, they appear as unavailable. Also, have you reinstalled the Mac software and rebuilt the desktop of the volume that contains the files? DESKTOP.AFP may be either corrupt or missing, and you'll have to rebuild it.

Tech Tip: Mac files have two parts (a data fork and a resource fork), and they support long names (40 characters). If your tape backup software recognizes only DOS file attributes, then you won't be able to back up and restore Mac files. In general, not all tape backup solutions can recognize the full Mac name, and they don't always tell you when they fail. Call the publisher of your backup software for the truth!

How do I rebuild the Macintosh volume desktop?

First mount the volume from the Macintosh and have rights to it. Then use the following procedure:

1. Unload AFP at the server console.
2. Type **Load AFP CDT**.
3. Log in from a Macintosh as supervisor.
4. From the Macintosh workstation, mount each volume, holding down the COMMAND and OPTION keys.

From this point, you will be prompted to rebuild each volume of the desktop.

How do I install Macintosh name space on a volume?

At the server, type **Load MAC.NAM** on the command line. (You can also add this line to STARTUP.NCF. This will provide Macintosh name space each time the server is booted.) Then, still at the server, type the following statement on the command line:

ADD NAME SPACE MACINTOSH TO VOLUME *volumename*

The command has to be typed once only. The name space is permanent unless VREPAIR is run.

Tech Tip: Name space must always be loaded before a related volume will mount.

If Macs are no longer in use on the network, can name space be removed?

Macintosh name space is the place where NetWare stores the resource fork of a Macintosh file. If no Macs are in use, there's no reason for maintaining Macintosh name space, and it can be removed. Name space can only be removed by running VREPAIR, as described in the following question and answer section.

How do I remove Macintosh name space from my server?

Use the following procedure to remove Macintosh name space:

1. Get all users of the Mac volume off the system.
2. Back up the disk.
3. Unmount the Mac volume.
4. Load VREPAIR.NLM.
5. Use ALT-ESC to switch back to the system console.

6. Load V_MAC.NLM to load Macintosh name space support for VREPAIR.

7. Select the option to remove name space, and confirm your request as needed.

VREPAIR will remove Macintosh name space. All files will remain on the system physically, but will only be accessible as DOS files. Make sure you also remove the LOAD statement for Macintosh name space from AUTOEXEC.NCF.

Whenever I log in through the Chooser, the message, "Save Name and Password" appears. Is there a way to disable this?

Yes. At the file server console when loading AFP, type **LOAD AFP ENCRYPT.** This disables the SET PASSWORD button in the Chooser. You must be using the NetWare UAM on the Macintosh.

What does NetWare mean by the message, "ATPS: Fatal queue error"?

Your AppleTalk Print Services queues or the print server may be corrupt. Use the following procedure to correct the situation. These steps should re-create the queues and print server automatically.

1. At the file server, unload ATPS.

2. Go to a workstation and log in as a supervisor equivalent.

3. Load PCONSOLE.

4. Delete the Macintosh print queues and then the Macintosh print server, ATPS_PSRVR, as shown here:

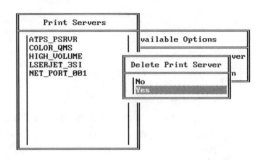

5. Go back to the file server and reload ATPS.

What does NetWare mean by the message, "0.0.0 atalk warning:atp returned error 60 on opencon reply. Severity one"?

A packet was sent but not received. If this problem happens often, there is probably a bad NIC card on the LAN. If it happens only occasionally, it is a timing problem, which will be corrected when the next packet is sent. Bad cabling on the Macintosh segment might also be the culprit. Is this Localtalk or Ethertalk? Is the card in the server used for other protocols? Is it a buffered card? All of these issues may affect the card's ability to respond to packet requests.

How can I see a print queue from a Mac?

To view a print queue created in PCONSOLE with a Macintosh, edit the ATPS.CFG file and add the following line:

-O *printserver queuename* -WB -L -F APPLWNT

After you add the line, unload and reload ATPS.NLM to make the changes take effect.

How can I recover a deleted Mac file?

If a Mac user accidentally deletes a file, it may be difficult to recover with the SALVAGE command. When a

Macintosh file is deleted, the resource forks to the file are also deleted (unlike a DOS file). After running SALVAGE, a DOS user will be able to see a DOS file, but a Mac user cannot see the Mac file. To attempt to recover a Mac file, you must rebuild the Mac desktop and try to rebuild the resource forks.

OS/2

What version of the NetWare Requester do I need for IBM OS/2 2.1?

The NetWare Requester (the NetWare Workstation for OS/2) version 2.01 will provide the most reliable connection between a NetWare file server and IBM OS/2 version 2.1.

Tech Tip: If you're using ODINSUP.SYS from the OS/2 2.0 NetWare Requester, and it does not allow IBM LAN Services to connect to the IBM host, move the IBM LAN Services drivers below the NetWare Requester section in CONFIG.SYS on the OS/2 workstation.

Is there a system login script for OS/2?

There are separate system login scripts for DOS machines and OS/2 machines. Both scripts are stored as text files in the SYS:PUBLIC directory. The DOS login script is called NET$LOG.DAT. The OS/2 login script is called NET$LOG.OS2.

Does the OS/2 Requester allow search drive mappings?

No. OS/2 does not support changes to its master environment after boot-up. Only network drive mappings are supported. You must add to the path any drive mappings you create.

When running NPRINT.EXE from an OS/2 machine, what does NetWare mean by the following message: "You have no rights to print files from this directory"?

This is a known problem with early versions of NPRINT and the OS/2 2.01 requester. The version of NPRINT.EXE dated 6/17/93 resolves this issue, and it is available on NetWire.

Print Services

The need for shared printing services is arguably more responsible than any other factor for the growth of LAN technology. The appearance of low-end laser printers capable of producing near-typeset-quality documents set the microcomputing world on fire during the mid-1980s. Though these devices were radically less expensive than their counterparts for mid-range and mainframe systems, their $3,000 to $5,000 price tag fueled the need for shared printing services.

Printing is still the most popular single shared service on a network, and thus printing problems are among the most important to solve for the user community. Until several years ago, many of the more innovative printing solutions, such as remote printers, were supplied by third-party vendors. Novell has now filled the niche somewhat, through upgrades to NetWare. Multimedia output from PC-based production sources is more and more widely used today, and so the typical LAN increasingly will include color printers and other sophisticated output devices. As this occurs, network administrators must be tuned to the rising demand for their networks' resources.

FRUSTRATION BUSTERS!

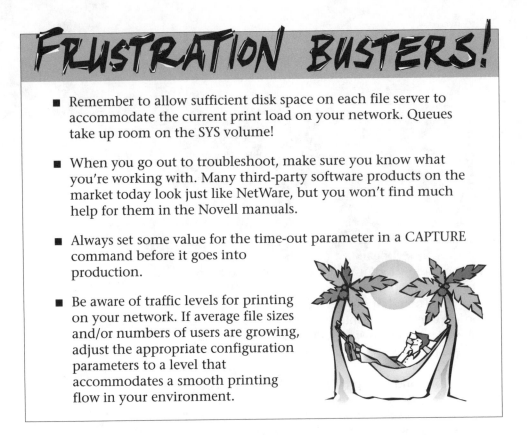

- Remember to allow sufficient disk space on each file server to accommodate the current print load on your network. Queues take up room on the SYS volume!

- When you go out to troubleshoot, make sure you know what you're working with. Many third-party software products on the market today look just like NetWare, but you won't find much help for them in the Novell manuals.

- Always set some value for the time-out parameter in a CAPTURE command before it goes into production.

- Be aware of traffic levels for printing on your network. If average file sizes and/or numbers of users are growing, adjust the appropriate configuration parameters to a level that accommodates a smooth printing flow in your environment.

I'm trying to print from Harvard Graphics for DOS, but the output splits onto two pages. What's the problem?

The queue is timing out and issuing a form feed to the printer. Use the TI parameter in the CAPTURE command to increase the period of time CAPTURE waits for data before it assumes the print job is complete. For a PostScript printer, this interval should be about 60 seconds.

It's also possible that your printer has insufficient memory. This will depend on the size and resolution of the image you're trying to print. In this case, you must add more memory to the printer, or try sending the output to another device that has more memory. It takes about 1MB of memory for an HP laser printer to image a 300-dpi black-and-white graphic image, and over 6MB for a color image on a QMS or Tektronics color printer.

Tech Tip: To set an infinite time-out, set it to zero. This is useful for testing purposes, but in practice you will have to exit the application to end the print job.

Why can't I print to the network through Windows?

The good news is that this problem is usually easy to solve once you know the cause. The bad news is that there are a lot of possible causes.

■ Do you have the right printer selected in your application? Go to the appropriate dialog box and verify the printer selection. You may be printing to the wrong printer or to the fax server.

■ Have you selected a network print queue? You can do this in several ways. One is to run the CAPTURE statement after you log in but before you enter Windows. Or you can use the Print Manager network options to select a queue on a file server to which you are attached, or to attach to a server and then select a queue. If you are connecting to a printer through a batch file after you are in Windows, make sure NetWare's share handles are enabled in Control Panel's network options.

Tech Tip: Try using NPRINT at the command line. This avoids depending on CAPTURE to redirect the ports, and allows you to send print jobs directly to the queues.

■ Is the printer driver installed under Windows the correct one? Do you have the most current driver for the printer? Is the driver corrupt?

■ Has Print Manager been disabled? If not, has someone deleted your print job from the queue, or has the queue been halted?

If the answers to all the foregoing questions are satisfactory, check to see if you can print to the network at all. Go to a DOS prompt and type the following line:

    COPY CONFIG.SYS LPT*x*

where *x* is the number of the LPT port to which you capture. If your workstation is talking to the network properly, a copy of your CONFIG.SYS will go to the printer. If this fails, make sure your parallel port has been properly redirected to the network. To do this, type **CAPTURE SHOW** at the command line. This lists all of your printer ports and shows their current status.

- If you find you can successfully print through DOS, then you may have a shell problem. Check NETX to see if it is version 3.26 or higher.

- Check IPX to see if it is version 3.10 or higher.

- Check Windows Setup (select the Windows Setup icon in the Main program group). The Network line should be set to Novell NetWare (shell versions 3.26 and above). If it isn't, select Options from the menu bar, and in the Options menu choose Change System Settings. Select version 3.26 or above from the list, save the setting, restart Windows, and try to print again.

Do printers take up a connection to my server?

It depends on how you set up your print server(s). Loading PSERVER.EXE on a dedicated workstation occupies a user connection, whereas loading PSERVER.NLM at the server console does not. In addition, a printer set up using RPRINTER.EXE on a non-dedicated workstation does not use a connection.

Can NetWare support a single PostScript printer for use by both Macintosh and DOS machines?

Yes. You need to define the printer properly to Novell, using PRINTDEF. Use PSTSCRPT.PDF to create an appropriate form for the text jobs from the DOS machines.

Tech Tip: It is important to decide how you are going to attach the printers. Macintosh PostScript printers are attached to Localtalk or Ethertalk. With NetWare for Macintosh, you must configure a queue that can access these printers. PostScript printers attached to the serial or parallel ports on the NetWare server may not be available to the Macintosh user.

When it's unplugged in the middle of a print job, the network printer behaves inconsistently. Sometimes the job resumes when the printer comes back on-line, but at other times the job is lost. What's going on?

When a printer is accidentally unplugged, the difference in its action when it comes back on line depends on the amount of memory in the printer. This, in turn, determines how quickly the entire print job spools to the printer. NetWare keeps a copy of a print queue file until all pages of a document are sent to the printer and they have been accepted. When an unplugged printer comes back up and the job resumes, it means the printer had not received all pages when communications failed. NetWare had not deleted the queue file, and it was reprinted immediately when the printer was brought back on line. If the print job does not resume, it means the entire job had already been transferred to the printer's memory, and the print queue file had been deleted by NetWare at the time of the failure. Thus, no attempt is made to reprint that job.

I have set the Copies field in the Microsoft Word Print dialog to 2, but each time I send the job to the printer, it creates 6 copies. What's wrong?

Use CAPTURE /SH to check the settings of your CAPTURE command—it probably has Copies set at 3. The result is that it prints the two copies from Word three times (2 x 3 = 6). Reset the CAPTURE command to 1 (the default), and the problem will go away. To set the session, type the following statement at the command line:

CAPTURE S=*servername* Q=*queuename* C=*number of copies*

You can use the PRINTCON utility to make this change permanent. Just delete the existing default print configuration.

When I load PSERVER.NLM, why does NetWare display the message, "Abend: Invalid OpCode processor exception running command console process"?

This error indicates bad hardware somewhere. It's probably the network card, but it could be related to bad memory, as well. Check the server for possible hardware trouble. Also, be sure you have the latest PSERVER.NLM for your version of NetWare.

What are the required parameters for a CAPTURE statement?

Required parameters for CAPTURE depend on the current environment. If a user has a default print job defined, the only required parameter is the job name, for example:

CAPTURE J=*jobname*

Following is a list of all parameters for CAPTURE:

CAPTURE Parameter	Purpose
SH (Show)	Displays the current status of LPT ports.
NOTI (Notify)	Returns a message to indicate when data has been printed. (This parameter is disabled by default.)
NNOTI (No Notify)	Returns no notification after data has been printed. (This parameter is enabled by default.)
TI=*n* (Timeout)	Defines the length of time the network will wait for a print job. Replace *n* with a number from 1 to 1,000 for the number of seconds to wait after the application last writes to a file before the data is sent to the network printer. (The default is 0, or timeout disabled.)
A (Autoendcap)	Sends data to the network printer when you enter or exit an application. (This parameter is enabled by default.)
NA (No Autoendcap)	Prevents data from being sent to the network printer or file when you enter or exit an application.
L=*n* (Local)	Specifies which of your workstations' LPT ports to capture. Replace *n* with 1, 2, or 3. (The default is 1.)

CAPTURE Parameter	Purpose
S=*server* (Server)	Indicates which file server will handle the print job.
Q=*queuename* (Queue)	Indicates the print queue to which the data will be sent.
CR=*path* (Create)	Specifies the name of the path and file where you want to store data.
J=*jobconfiguration* (Job)	Indicates the name of the job configuration, as defined in PRINTCON.
F=*form* or *n* (Form)	Specifies the name (*form*) or number (*n*) of the form you wish to use, as defined in PRINTDEF.
C=*n* (Copies)	Specifies the number of copies (1 to 999) you wish to print. (The default is 1.)
T=*n* (Tabs)	Specifies the number of characters (1 to 8) in a tab stop. (The default is 8.)
NT (NoTabs)	Ensures that tab characters arrive at the printer unchanged.
NB (NoBanner)	Suppresses the banner page.
NAM=*name* (Name)	Indicates the text that will appear in the upper part of the banner page. (The default is the user login name.)
B=*bannername* (Banner)	Indicates the text that will appear in the lower part of the banner page. (The default is LST:.)
FF (Form Feed)	Enables a form feed after the print job is completed.
NFF (No Form Feed)	Suppresses the form feed.
K (Keep)	Directs the file server to keep all data received from a workstation until no more data is sent or the workstation is disconnected, at which time the data is sent to the network printer.

What does NetWare mean by the message, "Not ready error writing device PRN"?

This may occur when you print to a file larger than 12K using a CAPTURE statement like this one:

```
CAPTURE NB NFF TI=1 CR=TEST.DST
```

If you increase the timeout (TI) parameter to 6 or greater, the problem disappears. Whenever the time-out limit is reached, NetWare sends an end-of-file marker. Because the timeout is so short in this example, the drive does not have time to close the file before NetWare starts sending the data again. Thus the file appears to be in use and the data cannot be written to it.

How can I create a standard print job configuration for the entire network?

You can create a default print job configuration without having to copy the file to each user individually. Log in to the network as supervisor and follow these steps:

1. Type **PRINTCON** at the command line, and create a global print job as shown in Figure 7-1.

2. Exit PRINTCON, and save the print job file.

3. Copy PRINTCON.DAT from FS/SYS:MAIL\0000001 to the public directory.

4. Flag the file as Shareable Read Only.

```
                Edit Print Job Configuration "Global"

Number of copies:     1          Form name:        Global
File contents:        Byte stream  Print banner:     Yes
Tab size:                         Name:
Suppress form feed:   No           Banner name:
Notify when done:     No

Local printer:        1           Enable timeout:   No
Auto endcap:          Yes         Timeout count:

File server:          GULAG-ARCH
Print queue:          SMASH
Print server:         WEASEL
Device:               Okidata Laserline 6
Mode:                 (Re-initialize)
```

FIGURE 7-1   Defining a print job with PRINTCON

5. Execute the following SMODE commands:

```
SMODE Z:PCONSOLE.EXE 5
SMODE Z:CAPTURE.EXE 5
SMODE Z:NPRINT.EXE 5
```

SMODE is a utility that changes the search mode for a program. These commands need to be executed only once. SMODE 5 makes the utilities PCONSOLE, CAPTURE, and NPRINT search the default directory first and then the search drives.

6. Set up the CAPTURE statement using the following syntax:

JOB = *global name*

All users will now have the global print job as their default.

How can I allow users to send out print jobs, but suppress printing at a particular printer?

You can suppress printing at a particular printer by setting the following option in PCONSOLE (you must be a console operator to do this):

Servers Can Service Entries in Queue = No

To set this option, select Print Queue Information, then Queue Name, then Current Queue Status. When you want the jobs to print, set the option back to Yes.

NetWare 4.*x*

Why do I receive memory errors when executing a CAPTURE statement from a login script on a NetWare 4.*x* server?

The versions of LOGIN.EXE and CAPTURE.EXE that ship with NetWare 4.*x* require more memory than in previous versions of NetWare. Executing the CAPTURE command from a login script causes LOGIN and

CAPTURE to load simultaneously, potentially consuming all of the workstation's available memory. To prevent this, exit the login script to a batch file that runs CAPTURE, or run CAPTURE from the command line after logging in to the network.

What is the difference between RPRINTER and NPRINTER?

RPRINTER and NPRINTER have similar functions. They both allow network printers to connect and print from network nodes rather than from dedicated print servers. NPRINTER lets you specify a workstation on which to load NPRINTER, and is poll driven by default. RPRINTER is interrupt driven.

What does NetWare mean by the message, "Error 776"?

This message may appear if you are loading RPRINTER.EXE in a batch file to create a nondedicated print server. This error occurs when a new SPX session is created before the previous session has been broken. (SPX sessions are created whenever RPRINTER.EXE is loaded.) The most likely reasons for SPX not being broken are that the machine was warm-booted or that RPRINTER.EXE is being loaded into RAM more than once. If you are loading RPRINTER.EXE from a batch file, you may want to use the following routine. This routine loops through RPRINTER.EXE until the new SPX connection can be made, and then loads the print server.

```
echo off
:loop
rprinter printservername printer#
if errorlevel 1 goto loop
Echo Rprinter Loaded Successfully !!!
```

Tech Terror: Some versions of RPRINTER do not report the errorlevel 1 error. The symptom can be difficult for the end-user to detect, because the message reported by RPRINTER is ambiguous: It says that the printer is "running," when it actually isn't.

How can I connect a plotter to the network?

To connect a plotter to a NetWare file server, check the application you use to send plots, and be sure you can direct output to one of the local parallel ports. If you can, it means the software does not need to maintain handshaking with the printer. As with all graphics output, set up your CAPTURE command with the NoTabs parameter.

What does NetWare mean by the message, "file q_3492331.srv.TTS file length kept=0"?

This indicates a problem with printer queues. Run BINDFIX to synchronize the queues and binderies. Delete the queue, run BINDFIX again, and re-create the queue.

What causes garbled print jobs?

If print jobs are cut off or mixed up with other print jobs, it's because NetWare doesn't look for an end-of-job marker. Instead, it simply gives each job a time limit in which to complete printing. If you encounter problems printing a very large document, try increasing the timeout value in your CAPTURE statement (or wherever you have your printing configuration data). This will give the job more time to print. You can also use the statement TI=0 to suppress the timeout altogether—this can be helpful when printing to a PostScript printer. Another cause of garbled print jobs may be that you are sending the job with the wrong printer driver selected. For instance, if you have selected a PostScript driver and you output to an HP PCL printer, the results will be rather large and useless.

Part of my landscape print job outputs correctly, but the remainder prints as garbage characters on several pages. What happened?

This can be caused by specification of a character string longer than the default length of the print job's print header. Solve the problem by setting a longer length for the header parameter in the workstation's SHELL.CFG file, for example, PRINT HEADER=72.

What does NetWare mean by the message, "Getqueuejoblist returned error code of 156"?

If you receive this error when attempting to print, it usually indicates corruption of the print queues. First try running BINDFIX. If that does not solve the problem, delete the print queues and re-create them.

What does NetWare mean by the message, "Not enough SPX connections"?

You may receive this message while loading PSERVER. There are several things you can try to correct the error. First, increase the number of SPX connections in SHELL.CFG. Second, make sure the printer port you are using has a unique interrupt, because this message can also occur when another device (such as a NIC) is on the same interrupt. It is recommended that PCs running either PSERVER.EXE or RPRINTER.EXE set SPX CONNECTIONS to 60 in the SHELL.CFG or NET.CFG.

NetWare 3.*x*

Why do I see "Queue *queuename* does not exist on server *servername*" when I try to CAPTURE my LPT port to a queue?

Either you've mistyped the name of your print queue or file server, or the server you need may be down. Check your spellings, and ask the network administrator if the queue is available.

When working in a DOS application, my documents will not print until I exit the application. Why?

Using the AUTOENDCAP switch (/A) in the CAPTURE statement may cause print jobs not to print until the application is exited. Use the CAPTURE statement with a timeout to reset, for example:

CAPTURE Q=*queuename* TI=10

The TI value of 10 is a reasonable setting for a typical laser printer; 60 is good for a color printer.

How do I delete a print job from the network print queue?

If there are multiple queues on your network, first make sure you know which queue the job was sent to. Type **CAPTURE /SH** at the command line, and NetWare will display the name of the server and print queue to which your jobs are currently being sent.

Tech Terror: If you are a PCONSOLE operator, be careful in step 5 above—you can see other jobs in the queue and may delete them by mistake.

1. Start the PCONSOLE utility by typing **PCONSOLE** at the command line.

2. Select Change Current File Server, and then select the server to which the print job was sent.

3. Select Print Queue Information, and then select the name of the print queue.

4. Select Current Print Job Entries.

5. Highlight your print job in the list and press DEL. If your print job is not displayed in the list of current print jobs, the job is already at the printer and you cannot delete it.

6. Press ALT-F10 or ESC.

7. Select Yes to exit PCONSOLE.

Is there a way I can stop printing without having to go into PCONSOLE?

The PSC command can control network printers from the command line. This command can also be placed in a batch file, which is very useful for quickly changing forms or pausing the printer to realign paper. The syntax for the command is as follows:

PSC PS=*print server* P=*print number flaglist*

flaglist can be replaced with any one of the following values (caps indicate abbreviations): STATus, PAUse, ABort, STOp, STARt, Mark, FormFeed, MOunt Form=n, PRIvate, SHared, and CancelDown. The ABort option will cancel the current job and delete it from the queue.

What does NetWare mean by the message, "Capture requires a 2.10 or later shell in order to work"?

This message means you are using a Network shell version that does not support the CAPTURE command. You need to load a later version of the NetWare shell (2.1 or above).

In Windows, when I select Printers from Control Panel, the Network button is grayed out in the Connect dialog box, even though my workstation is connected to the network (I can see network drives in File Manager or in DOS). What's wrong?

If the Network button is unavailable, as shown here:

Connect	
NEC Silentwriter LC890	**OK**
Ports:	**Cancel**
LPT1: Local Port	Settings...
LPT2: Local Port Not Present	
LPT3: Local Port Not Present	Network...
COM1: Local Port	
COM2: Local Port Not Present	**Help**
Timeouts (seconds)	
Device Not Selected: 15	
Transmission Retry: 120	
☒ Fast Printing Direct to Port	

check the shell version you have specified within Windows Setup. This version number must match the shell version you are actually running. If it doesn't, correct it, and the Network button should become available.

I am running NPRINT.EXE from an OS/2 machine and I get the message, "You have no rights to print files from this directory." What does this mean?

This is a known bug with early versions of NPRINT and the OS/2 requester 2.01. The version of NPRINT.EXE dated 6/17/93 resolves this issue, and is available on NetWire.

Can Macs print to a plotter on the network through NetWare?

No. The drivers are not available for Macs.

What is the maximum size of a print buffer in NetWare?

The maximum size of a print buffer in NetWare is 255K.

Where does NetWare store the print job configuration files created in PRINTCON?

Print job configuration files are stored in a user's MAIL directory. If none exists, NetWare will use a configuration file in the public directory on the path.

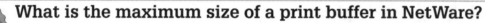

Why am I getting the message, "No more IPX sockets are available" on my print server?

The error refers to the sockets being used on the workstation. The default value for IPX Sockets in the SHELL.CFG is 20. Increasing that value should resolve the issue.

Does Windows support the use of RPRINTER?

Officially, no. Windows has some difficulty printing to a workstation running RPRINTER, although most of the time it will work. Try increasing the Transmission Retry setting in RPRINTER. Or you can open Control Panel, select Printers and then Connect in Windows, and change to LPT1. Also, make sure you are running the most current version of RPRINTER. It must be loaded before starting Windows, because RPRINTER is a TSR and uses an SPX network connection.

I am loading PSERVER.NLM at the file server, and the system asks for a password. If there is no password on the print server, how can I get past this?

The print server definition is corrupt or does not exist. You need to delete the print server definition and re-create it or create one in PCONSOLE.

1. Log in as supervisor, and load PCONSOLE.
2. Select Change Current File server, and then select the file server where the print server is loading.
3. Select Print Server Information, and then select the print server name.
4. Select Yes to delete the server name.
5. Re-create the print server configuration.
6. Reload the print server at the file server console.

How do I keep the banner page from printing out before each print job?

To stop the banner page from printing, add the /NB flag to the CAPTURE statement. Your capture statement might now look like this:

```
CAPTURE S=SERVER1 Q=HP4SI NB TI=10
```

What does NetWare mean by the message, "There are no more response buffers available"?

PSERVER.EXE is reporting that the print server's memory is low (this is a workstation, not a NetWare file server). Reboot the print server first, to see if it will clear itself. If not, you may want to consider upgrading the print server's memory.

What does NetWare mean by the message, "Network Spooler Error: (probably out of space on SYS:*volume*)"?

NetWare 3.11 requires that print jobs be temporarily stored in the SYS volume. This message can occur after sending a job to a network printer if there is not enough free space on the volume to spool the job, and the job is deleted.

Whenever I send something to the printer, my server abends with the error message, "Lost hardware interrupt." What's wrong?

This is a known bug in version 1.21 of PSERVER.NLM. Upgrade to version 1.21b. This patch is available on NetWire.

When a large job is printing, why does the server lock up and display "Abend: stack fault processor exception"?

This is a known problem with some versions of ISADISK.DSK, and can be resolved by loading ISADISK with the /b switch. The /b switch forces the ISADISK driver to act like the 3.10 ISADISK driver and checks the BIOS for drive information. Also, if you are using an IDE drive, you can utilize the newer IDE.DSK driver that Novell now ships with all versions of NetWare.

How can I check the status of a print server?

Use PCONSOLE to manage print operations. Print server information such as Print Server Version and Queue Service Modes is now shown on the screen. Follow these steps:

1. Run PCONSOLE.

2. From the Available Options menu, choose Print Server Information.

3. From the Print Servers menu, choose a print server.

4. From the Print Server Information menu, choose Print Server Status/Control.

5. Choose Server Info from the Print Server Status and Control menu shown here. (This choice is not available if the print server is inactive.)

```
┌─────────────────────────────────────┐
│ Print Server Status and Control     │
├─────────────────────────────────────┤
│ File Servers Being Serviced         │
│ Notify List for Printer             │
│ Printer Status                      │
│ Queues Serviced by Printer          │
│ Server Info                         │
└─────────────────────────────────────┘
```

How can I schedule a job for deferred printing?

To flag a job for deferred printing, you must catch or trap the job in the queue, as follows:

1. Run PCONSOLE.

2. Select Print Queue Information.

3. Choose the queue to which the job was sent.

4. Select Current Print Job Entries.

5. Highlight the print job you wish to defer and press ENTER.

6. Switch the "Defer printing" field to Yes, as shown in Figure 7-2.

7. Fill in the appropriate target date and time.

If the queue is empty when the job is first sent, you may have to disable all printing from that queue before sending the job, in order to catch it before it is spooled to the printer. To do this, use the following procedure:

1. Start PCONSOLE.

2. Select Print Queue Information from the Available Options menu.

3. Choose the queue to which the job was sent.

4. Select Current Queue Status.

5. Highlight the option "Servers can service entries in queue," and switch the field to No.

6. Press ESC to back out of and exit PCONSOLE.

7. Use NPRINT or CAPTURE to print the selected job.

Tech Tip: Remember to reset the "Servers can service entries in queue" option to Yes after the deferred job is trapped.

```
NetWare Print Console  V1.51                Wednesday  March 9, 1994  4:50 pm
                 User SUPERVISOR On File Server GULAG-ARCH Connection 1

                           Print Queue Entry Information

Print job:         1184              File size:        2994
Client:            SUPERVISOR[1]
Description:       LPT1 Catch
Status:            Ready To Be Serviced, Waiting For Print Server

User Hold:         No                Job Entry Date:   March 9, 1994
Operator Hold:     No                Job Entry Time:   4:49:28 pm
Service Sequence:  4

Number of copies:  1                 Form:             Global
File contents:     Byte stream       Print banner:     Yes
Tab size:                            Name:             SUPERVISOR
Suppress form feed: No               Banner name:
Notify when done:  No
                                     Defer printing:   Yes
Target server:     (Any Server)      Target date:      March 9, 1994
                                     Target time:      4:00:00 pm
```

FIGURE 7-2   Deferring a print job

Communications Services

On a network, communications is one of the most difficult areas to troubleshoot because there are so many factors to consider. When you stop to think about it, controlling problems in even single-user communications environments takes more time than other problem issues. To begin with, it's simply more difficult to find answers. Support personnel who are knowledgeable in communications are generally harder to come by than in more common and familiar areas such as printing or file services. Secondly, the types of available communications devices cover an extremely broad range, and many are nonstandard. For example, so many Hayes-compatible modems exist that it would be difficult to compile a list. And even if you could, you would never be sure of all the various protocols supported, though this information might be essential in diagnosing a communications problem on your network. Then there's the issue of what's happening on the other end. Some factors—such as line quality, or the receiving devices and protocols—are beyond your control or sometimes even your knowledge. Finally, communications devices and processes are extremely sensitive, so other changes in the network environment can fairly easily cause communications failures.

Now that you're prepared for the worst, you can start to build a strategy for success.

FRUSTRATION BUSTERS!

- Test and reset modems regularly.

- Reset communications servers after any important modification or event on the network.

- Make sure your lines aren't dead.

- Check for PC-related problems. Your server is also a PC, so don't overlook the obvious.

- Check available error logs.

I have a NACS communications server on my network, and I'm running ProComm for Networks, but I can't access the NACS server to dial-out. What's wrong?

For a workstation to access NACS services, the NASI interface is required. Make sure you run NASI.EXE prior to executing ProComm. Also, be sure you have named and selected the ports of the ACS; just loading the driver does not mean that a port has been selected. The ACS has a server name, a specific name(s), and a general name. The *server name* identifies the entire computer acting as the ACS, the *specific name* refers to a single individual port, and the *general name* refers to one or more ports on the ACS, as shown here:

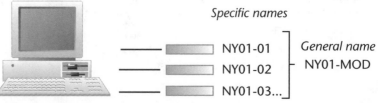

Server name
ALS_NY01

Specific names

NY01-01
NY01-02
NY01-03...

General name
NY01-MOD

What frame type supports IP packet protocol?

ETHERNET_II supports IP packet control.

Tech Tip: To change the frame type, you must be using ODI drivers. Monolithic drivers only support IPX. The default for the older ODI Ethernet shells was 802.3. The new ODI drivers and VLM client use 802.2, so you may have to set the 802.3 driver as well as the ETHERNET_II frame. This is done in NET.CFG. For example, add the line, **FRAME ETHERNET_802.3** under the link driver section.

NetWare 3.*x*

What are the latest versions of NACS and NASI?

Version 3.02D is the latest for NACS; for NASI, it's 3.02E. These versions solve some problems of compatibility between earlier versions of NACS and NASI 3.00, and other communications programs.

How many physical ports can a NACS support?

NACS version 2.09 can support up to 16 physical ports, and NACS 3.02 can support up to 32. These are assigned during configuration. You can establish a connection to any physical port.

I am having odd problems with my NACS. What are some of the possible causes?

The NACS is a very sensitive device. It depends on the correct operation of many other parts of the network. The list of possible trouble sources could go on for many pages, but here are some things to think about first:

- Make sure the correct modem cables are being used (see Table 8-1).
- Make sure the modems are on and that they are supported.

In/Out	PIN	Abbreviation	Function
Out	2	TXD	Transmit data
In	3	RXD	Receive data
Out	4	RTS	Request to send
In	5	CTS	Clear to send
In	6	DSR	Data set ready
Required	7	GND	Signal ground
In	8	DCD	Data carrier detect
Out	20	DTR	Data terminal ready

TABLE 8-1   Proper Modem Cable Pinouts for NACS

- Make sure the network adapter is correctly installed.

- Be aware that when you are connected to a port on the NACS, it's possible to change the modem settings in such a way to make the modem unusable.

- Make sure that you are using NACS version 2.09 or higher. You can get this in NOVA Library 9 on CompuServe.

- Check to see that you have met the minimum hardware requirements for your NACS server.

- Use only NASI-compliant communications applications (NACS will not support anything else).

- Do not use a shared memory network adapter. Each multi-port serial adapter must have its own 64K memory address that does not conflict with video cards, hard drives, controllers, NICs, or other hardware.

What causes the error that the NACS is not responding when using Crosstalk Mark IV?

If you select the NASI setting within Crosstalk's communications setup, you will be asked for a server name. The field appears to be asking for the NACS server name, but it is not. What it needs is either the specific or general name of a NACS port. If you enter the name of your NACS server, you will get this error. For details concerning the different names used by the ACS, refer to the first question in this chapter.

Why can't I upload with Ymodem protocol on my NACS?

Older versions of NASI can only write a data buffer of 498 bytes at a time, but they can read 512 bytes. Ymodem and Ymodem G both need 512 bytes for read and write buffers, causing the problem. To solve it, upgrade to NASI version 2.15 or above.

Can you use one modem in your file server for both NACS and GMHS?

Yes. In NACS version 3.*x*, the modem in the file server is only used for dialing out. The port is locked down by GMHS for incoming calls.

Does NetWare FLeX/IP or NetWare NFS support Trivial File Transport Protocol (TFTP)?

No. FLeX/IP—an NLM used to assist in UNIX connectivity—supports File Transport Protocol (FTP).

Tech Tip: FLeX/IP stands for File Transfer Protocol (F), Line Printer Daemon (L), and X Window support (X).

Can NASI be loaded high successfully?

Yes, if there is enough high memory available. NASI requires 51K. Be aware, however, that system performance may suffer when NASI is loaded high.

How do I use Kermit with a NACS?

First load NASI, then run Kermit. At a Kermit prompt, type **SET PORT NOVELL** (this assumes that the NACS is called Novell). Then type **C** and press ENTER. You should now see a NASI prompt and be able to specify one of the following terminal types:

VT320 (default)
Honeywell VIP7809
Heath-19
VT52
VT100
VT102
VT220
Tek4010

Does the GMHS asynchronous driver use ports directly, or must it go through a NACS?

Novell's Global Message Handling Service (GMHS) does not support NACS. For 2400 baud or less you must use a COM port. If you are going to use modems with higher transmission rates, in the server you must use a serial I/O adapter that has intelligent serial ports, such as a Digiboard. You can also set up an external serial gateway for use with GMHS, but this will require a second computer.

What do I need to do in order to run TCP/IP?

Novell NetWare 3.11 supports TCP/IP packets and routing at the server without any additional software, but you must make sure you have a frame type that supports TCP/IP. Following are the common transports and their frame types:

Topology	Frame Type
Ethernet	ETHERNET_II
Token Ring	TOKEN-RING_SNAP
ARCnet	No frame needs to be specified

When implementing the TCP/IP options with NetWare 3.11, you must remember to load the LAN driver that will receive TCP/IP packets with the ETHERNET_II packet frame type. If you do not load the driver with a frame type, NetWare will load the board to accept ETHERNET_802.3 packets only. Following are the commands to load the LAN driver and configure the frame type:

```
LOAD NE2000 PORT=300
INT=3
FRAME=ETHERNET_II
NAME=ETHER_TCP
```

This loads the NE2000 driver, interrupt 3, the ETHERNET_II frame type, and names the driver ETHER_TCP. The name is optional; it makes it easier to bind this frame type to a protocol.

When using NetWare 3.11 to route TCP/IP packets, you must add a FORWARD=YES statement when loading the TCP/IP protocol. To do this, first load a LAN driver with the correct frame type, then load the TCP/IP protocol with the FORWARD option, and then bind the driver to the protocol. For example:

```
LOAD TOKEN NAME=IPX-TOKEN
BIND IPX TO IPX-TOKEN
     NET=1
LOAD NE2000
     PORT=300
     NT=3
     FRAME=ETHERNET_II
     NAME=ETH-IP
LOAD TOKEN FRAME=TOKEN-RING_SNAP
     NAME=IP-TOKEN
LOAD TCPIP
     FORWARD=YES
BIND IP TO ETH-IP ADDR=129.1.0.5
```

(In the last line above, the number following ADDR= should be your Internet address.) In this case, TCP/IP packets are routed from the Ethernet segment to the Token Ring segment.

Tech Tip: To run TCP/IP, you will also need a copy of LAN Workplace for DOS or Windows, or another NetWare-compatible TCP/IP package. These packages contain the TCP/IP utilities needed to add the TCP/IP protocol to a NetWare workstation. Each package will have specific instructions for installation.

Utilities

Like most operating systems, NetWare is a collection of executable programs used to manage an environment; it is not a single application. From this point of view, all NetWare programs are utilities. The questions in this chapter don't fall into any clear cut application category, yet they do address issues that commonly occur in administrating a NetWare environment.

Is there a command-line utility that provides a quick way of copying files across the network?

The NCOPY utility works just like the DOS XCOPY command, but is much faster. Since NCOPY is a NetWare utility, it accesses the NetWare FAT and DET stored in the server's RAM. NCOPY provides a much safer means of copying files across the network because it utilizes read-after-write verification. Also, NCOPY succeeds with open files, whereas XCOPY fails. This is very useful on the network because files that you want to copy are often in use by someone else on the system.

The syntax for NCOPY is as follows:

NCOPY *d:filename* TO *d:filename* /*switches*

Here is a list of the NCOPY switches:

Switch	Description
/?	Previews a list of all the switches available.
/S	Copies subdirectories.
/E	Creates empty directories on the target.
/F	Copies sparse files.
/C	Copies without preserving file attributes.
/I	Displays a warning message if any attributes cannot be copied.
/V	Invokes read-after-write verification.
/A	Copies files that have the archive bit set.
/M	Copies files with the archive bit set and turns off the archive bit of the source file; this is useful when using NCOPY as part of a backup routine.

Is there a way to attach to servers, remap drives, and access print queues without exiting Windows?

Through the Windows File Manager, you can attach to servers and map drives using the Network Connections option on the Disk menu. In Print Manager, you can access print queues through the Network Connections option (see Figure 9-1), and connect them to printers defined in Windows (see Figure 9-2).

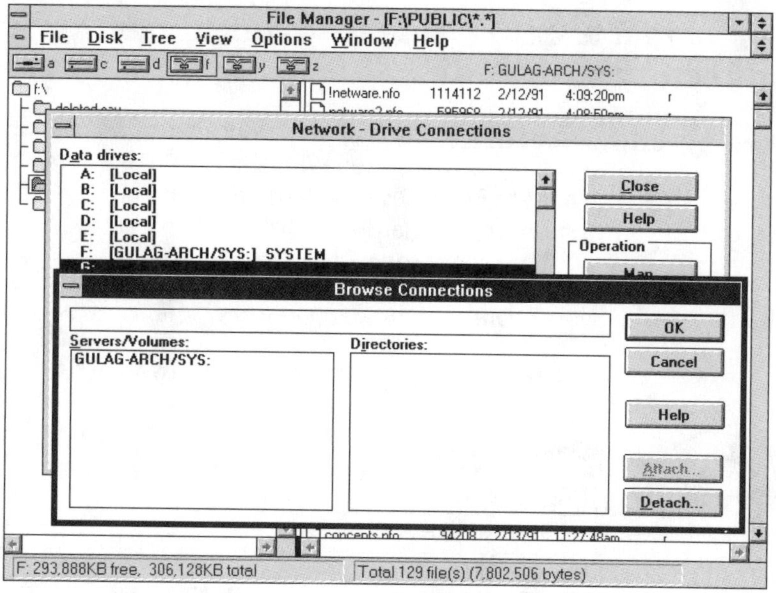

FIGURE 9-1   The Network Connections dialog box

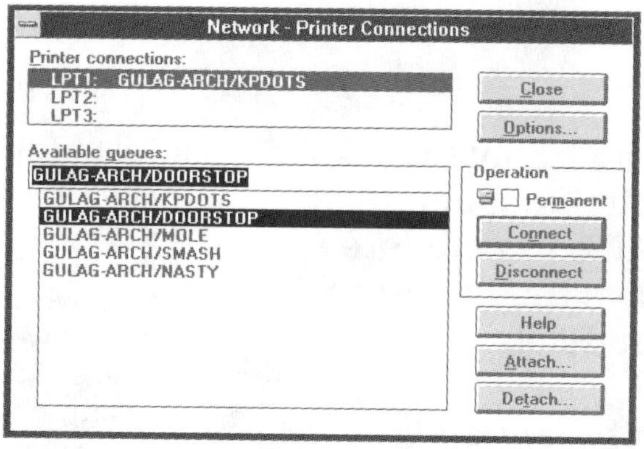

FIGURE 9-2   The Network - Printer Connections dialog box

Is there a way to locate files quickly within a NetWare directory structure?

The NDIR utility is an excellent means of locating files. For example, when used with the /SUB parameter, NDIR will search all subdirectories and pause as it finds the specified files. NDIR supports standard DOS wildcard characters.

The syntax for NDIR is as follows:

NDIR *filename.ext* /*switches*

Here is a list of the most common switches for NDIR:

Switch	Description
/Help	Displays a complete list of options.
/SUB	Searches subdirectories.
/H	Displays hidden files.
/SY	Displays system files.
/DATES	Displays dates the specified file was last modified, last archived, last accessed, and created.
/LONG	Displays name space names.
/RIGHTS	Displays inherited and effective rights.
/SIZE	Limits the scope of the search.
/SORT	Determines the display order of output; for example, by owner or size.

How can I prevent someone from using SALVAGE to undelete a sensitive file I want to remain deleted?

By adding the file attribute for Purge (P), you flag the file for permanent (nonsalvageable) deletion. Use the FLAG utility to change the attribute on the file; when this file is deleted, no trace of it will remain. Here is an example of the FLAG command with the Purge option:

```
FLAG SYS:/APPS/DATA/INVOICE.001 P
```

You can also run the PURGE utility after deleting files, and any salvageable files will be deleted.

Tech Terror: Use PURGE with extreme caution. Once a file is purged, your backups are the only recourse you have in the event you need the material again!

How can I get a list of users currently connected to a file server?

The USERLIST, MONITOR, and SESSION utilities all provide this information.

For USERLIST, you must be attached to the server whose user list you want to view. Type the following statement at the command line:

USERLIST *fileserver*

where *fileserver* specifies the name of a server other than your default.

On a NetWare 4.*x* server, the equivalent command is

NLIST *user*

The available switches for USERLIST are as follows:

Switch	Description
/A	Lists network addresses.
/O	Displays object-type information.
/C	Causes the output to scroll continuously.

Another way to view the server connections is to type **LOAD MONITOR** at the console prompt. Once you're in MONITOR, select Connection Information. This displays all connections to the server, including machines with the NetWare shell loaded that are not logged in, and any print servers attached to the server, as shown in Figure 9-3.

The last alternative for viewing network connections is to use the SESSION utility and select User List as an option.

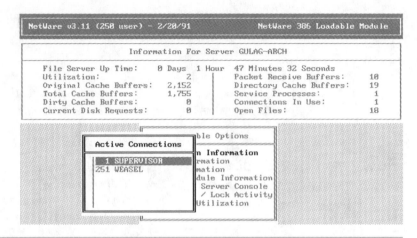

```
NetWare v3.11 (250 user) - 2/20/91          NetWare 386 Loadable Module

                    Information For Server GULAG-ARCH

   File Server Up Time:    0 Days  1 Hour  47 Minutes 32 Seconds
   Utilization:                      2     Packet Receive Buffers:      10
   Original Cache Buffers:       2,152     Directory Cache Buffers:     19
   Total Cache Buffers:          1,755     Service Processes:            1
   Dirty Cache Buffers:              0     Connections In Use:           1
   Current Disk Requests:            0     Open Files:                  18
```

```
                                        ble Options
         Active Connections
                                     n Information
           1 SUPERVISOR              rmation
         251 WEASEL                  mation
                                     dule Information
                                      Server Console
                                     / Lock Activity
                                     Utilization
```

FIGURE 9-3   Active network connections as shown in MONITOR

What is SESSION used for?

The SESSION utility can be used for the following tasks:

- Changing current file servers
- Viewing or temporarily changing drive mappings
- Temporarily changing, creating, or deleting search drives
- Viewing groups on the network
- Choosing a default drive
- Listing user information
- Sending messages to users and groups

Which utilities allow me to add a user to a file server?

There are four utilities that let you add users to a NetWare file server:

- SYSCON allows you to add one user at a time.
- With MAKEUSER, you can set up a script file to add and delete multiple users. This very powerful command is

extremely useful when you need to attend to many users on a regular basis.

■ USERDEF lets you create multiple users, simple login scripts, home directories, minimum login/password security, and print job configurations. You can pick from predefined templates for user profiles.

■ NWUSER replaces USERDEF in NetWare 4.*x* and will create users, home directories, and a simple user login script.

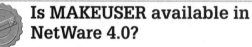

NetWare 4.*x*

Is MAKEUSER available in NetWare 4.0?

No. In NetWare 4.0, UIMPORT performs the same functions that MAKEUSER performed in previous versions. The difference between these utilities is that MAKEUSER is menu driven, while UIMPORT is run at the command line. The syntax for UIMPORT is as follows:

UIMPORT *controlfile datafile*

where *controlfile* is the name of a file containing instructions on loading data into the directory, and *datafile* is the name of a comma delimited ASCII file containing attribute values.

Since upgrading to VLMs, I can't run NETADMIN.EXE? Why?

It means there aren't enough file handles available. VLMs ignore the FILES statement in NET.CFG. Increase the FILES parameter in CONFIG.SYS to at least 100, and NETADMIN.EXE will work.

Can I use SYSCON to administer my NetWare 4.x server?

In NetWare 4.*x*, SYSCON can be used to administer bindery emulation users only. The replacements for SYSCON in NetWare 4.*x* are NETADMIN (for DOS) and NWADMIN (for Windows), and these must be used to administer NDS users.

When I use NWADMIN or NETADMIN to create an object, NetWare displays a message that the object cannot be created, along with an FD6D or 659 code. Why?

This indicates a problem with your server time. On a single-server network, it means the creation time of a directory is somehow later than the server time. On a multiserver network, this error means server times are not synchronized. You will be able to accomplish certain tasks even though time is not synchronized; but other tasks, such as creating objects, result in error messages. To correct this problem, change the server time to the correct time and check it periodically. If you are on a multiserver network, your server time should automatically synchronize to network time.

What utility would I use to repair a damaged NDS database?

The DSREPAIR utility checks and repairs the partitions and replicas stored on the server where the utility is run. It also checks and repairs NDS records, and file system bindery problems such as invalid trustee IDs.

How can I tell whose Network ID is being used at a particular workstation?

To find out who is logged in to a particular network workstation, use WHOAMI at the command line of the workstation in question. This command lists the file servers to which the station is connected, the IDs in use, the connection number, the login time and date, and the version of NetWare being used by that server.

Tech Tip: USERLIST /A will display a list of users that are currently logged in on a server, and what station they are logged in at.

 ## How can I tell how much network disk space is available to me?

To find out how much disk space is available to a specific user on a specific drive, type the CHKVOL command at the command line, in the following syntax:

CHKVOL *file server name/volume name*

This displays the following data:

```
Total Volume Space
Space in use by files
Space in use by deleted files
Space available from deleted files
Space remaining on volume
Space available to the person logged on at that workstation
```

 ## How can I display space information about a particular network directory?

To display information about available space for a specific network directory, change to that directory and type **CHKDIR** at the command line. This displays volume space information, the amount of space available to the user, and the amount of space being used by files in that directory.

NetWare 3.*x*

 ## When I run SYSCON, some functions work fine, but others result in errors. What's wrong?

Are you the administrator? Some of the functions in SYSCON are reserved for supervisor equivalents, and you may not have the appropriate security privileges to use all of them.

Are there other problems on the network that might indicate trouble in the area in which SYSCON is supposed to be operating? Are people having difficulty logging in? Are print queues or other files disappearing? Could a volume be failing? There can be many causes for this problem. In extreme cases, the NetWare bindery has been corrupted. If so, you can try running BINDFIX, but this does not always fix the problem. A corrupt bindery may require restoration.

Tech Tip: Before running BINDFIX or VREPAIR, make sure you have at least two full backups of the server. If BINDFIX or VREPAIR work, there were problems with either the bindery or the volume you ran VREPAIR on. Often it's a lot less trouble to take 20 minutes and run through a checklist of common problems than it is to spend the rest of the day restoring the server. VREPAIR takes time, depending on the size of the drive.

The rights I assign to users with SYSCON version 3.62 disappear the next time I edit the user, but they appear correctly in FILER. Is this a known problem?

Yes. Assigned rights may not appear correctly in SYSCON version 3.62. The problem was resolved with SYSCON version 3.68, and this patch is available on NetWire.

When I define a user as a group member, the user appears in the group member list in SYSCON, but the group name does not appear in the Groups Belonged To option. What is going on?

This is a known bug in BINDFIX 3.52, which shipped with NetWare 3.11. BINDFIX.EXE 3.53 fixes the problem, and it checks all members of the group for consistency. To receive BINDFIX 3.53, the patch is available on NetWire, or you can download patch #1566 from Corporate Software's Electronic Services System bulletin board, or call Corporate Software's Product Support Hotline.

Tech Tip: Version 3.53 of BINDFIX was compiled using the large memory model, so it does not run out of memory when checking for duplicate objects or duplicate properties. It also corrects a library-linking problem in the previous version.

Why does USERLIST report no users, though some are actually logged in to the network?

Make sure you are logged in to the network on at least one file server. If you are attached but not logged in, USERLIST will execute, but it cannot determine who is logged in unless you are. Also, USERLIST is server specific and only displays users of the designated server. For example, the command USERLIST SERVER1 displays a list of users on Server1 if you are logged in to Server1.

What is VREPAIR and when should I run it?

VREPAIR is an NLM used to correct volume problems or to remove name space entries from FATs and DETs. You might consider running VREPAIR, as shown in Figure 9-4, in the following instances:

- A power failure has corrupted the volume.
- When the file server boots, the file server console displays a mirroring error.
- A hardware failure has either prevented a volume from mounting or caused a disk read error.
- The file server console displays memory errors and cannot mount a volume after a name space has been added to the volume. You must either add more memory to the file server, or remove the newly added name space with VREPAIR.

Tech Terror:
VREPAIR takes time to run and some of its processes are not reversible, so use this utility with caution.

```
Current Vrepair Configuration:

    Quit If A Required VRepair Name Space Support NLM Is Not Loaded

    Write Only Changed Directory And FAT Entries Out To Disk

    Keep Changes In Memory For Later Update

Options:

    1. Remove Name Space support from the volume

    2. Write All Directory And FAT Entries Out To Disk

    3. Write Changes Immediately To Disk

    0. Return To Main Menu

    Enter your choice:
```

FIGURE 9-4   The menu for the VREPAIR utility

After running VREPAIR, I still get server errors on a volume. What's wrong?

VREPAIR often takes several passes to correct all the errors it encounters. If you have run VREPAIR several times and the same errors are turning up, there may be other issues involved. For instance, you can get errors if the volume is full or there are too many directory entries (depending on the size of the disk). These problems can be corrected through simple housekeeping. Logical partition map damage to the disk will also cause errors that you may be able to correct with a third-party disk diagnostics program, such as Ontrack Netutils or Netutils 3. You may have to re-create the volume and/or restore the data from your backup tapes. This means bringing the network down and initializing the disk.

When should I run BINDFIX?

Run BINDFIX when you think data in the bindery has been corrupted. BINDFIX corrects the following problems:

- Inability to delete a user's name

- Inability to modify a user's rights

- Inability to modify a user's password

- The error, "Unknown Server," which occurs during print spooling, even though you are spooling to a default server

- Error messages referring to the bindery that are displayed at the file server console

I ran BINDFIX after I detected errors in the bindery, but the errors are still present afterwards. What's wrong?

Did you bring down the server and restart it? The changes made by BINDFIX are not loaded until the server is downed and brought back up again. Also, make sure you have the proper versions of utilities such as SYSCON. These change frequently, so be sure to check NetWire.

Tech Terror: VREPAIR and BINDFIX are somewhat indiscriminate and time-consuming. Once you've got one of these utilities started, plan to be there for a while. They will fix anything and everything they can find to fix—not just the problem you thought you had. Also, when they fail, these utilities don't tell you much about what happened. Before running one of these utilities, always make a backup of the volume you're working on. Call Ontrack at 612-937-2121; they can sometimes restore the data and send you floppies or a tape of a disk you send them. This is a last-resort service, but it may save your feathers.

Does NetWare 3.11 provide any diagnostic tools for working with router and server problems across subnets?

Yes. The TRACK, RESET ROUTER, and DISPLAY SERVERS utilities all can help.

Invoke TRACK by typing **TRACK ON** at the server console. This gives you route information, server information, and workstation connection requests, in the form of

```
Get Nearest Server
```

and

```
Give Nearest Server
```

statements on the screen. To exit TRACK, type **TRACK OFF** at the server console.

RESET ROUTER causes the server to send broadcasts to all known servers in its routing table. When you turn TRACK on, RESET ROUTER will display responses from all the server objects on the network. To execute this utility, just type **RESET ROUTER** at the command line.

The DISPLAY SERVERS and DISPLAY NETWORKS commands will also show what NetWare devices are on the network.

When running BINDFIX, why do I get the message, "Error: Unable To Create Temporary File TMP$VAL.TMP. Attempt To Fix Bindery Was Unsuccessful"?

This error can result if you are running VLMs with a NET.CFG file that includes a FILE HANDLES statement set to 100, and a CONFIG.SYS file that includes a FILES statement set to 25. Reset the FILES statement in CONFIG.SYS to 50 by adding the line FILES=50 to the file, or changing the value for the FILES parameter.

What is NVER?

The NVER command is useful when you need to know the version and configuration for a LAN driver or file server. NVER supplies version information for NETBIOS, IPX, SPX, LAN driver, SHELL, DOS, and OS (its version and user pack). To run NVER, just type **NVER** at the command line.

Why isn't NBACKUP available under NetWare 3.12?

Though the NBACKUP command is listed as available in the NetWare 3.12 Buyer's Guide, the actual files are missing—they were left out of the shipped version. You can download NBCKUP.EXE from the LIB4 area of NetWire on CompuServe.

What SFT features are available in NetWare 3.12?

There are seven System Fault Tolerance (SFT) features in NetWare 3.*x*:

- The *Transaction Tracking System (TTS)* protects database applications from corruption by backing out incomplete transactions that result from a failure in a network component.

- Disk mirroring requires at least two physical network volumes. *Mirroring* is the duplication of data from the NetWare partition of one hard disk to the network partition of another hard disk. The disks are on the same channel (same disk controller), so if the primary drive fails, the secondary drive activates automatically.

- *Disk duplexing* is similar to mirroring, but each hard disk is on a separate channel and disk controller. This feature provides a further level of fault tolerance: If one controller fails, you can still access the secondary drive.

- *UPS monitoring* allows you to monitor an uninterruptible power supply attached to the file server.

- The *Hot Fix* feature redirects faulty data blocks from the main storage area to a small area designated as the Hot Fix Redirection area. This prevents data from being written to a bad storage area on the hard drive.

- With *read-after-write verification*, data remains in memory when it is written to the hard disk. The data in memory is then compared to the data on the hard disk. If the data matches, NetWare releases the data from memory. If not, the block location is tagged as bad, and Hot Fix redirects the data to a good block in the Hot Fix area.

- Duplicate copies of the FAT and DET remain on the NetWare partition at all times.

How can I print a hardcopy of the SECURITY report?

Redirect the output to a file, using the following syntax:

SECURITY > *filename.ext*

You can then use a text editor or word processor to format and print the file.

After I access my file server through RCONSOLE, how do I exit and return to my workstation screen?

There are two ways to exit from RCONSOLE. You can

- press SHIFT and ESC at the same time, which displays a menu asking you if you want to quit the remote console session

- press the gray * key on the numeric keypad all the way to the right side of your keyboard. This displays a menu with six options, one of which is to end the remote session

Tech Tip: When using RCONSOLE to access the server console, you cannot use the ALT-ESC key sequence to scroll through the loaded NLMs. Instead, you must use the + key on the numeric keypad.

Why is IBM$RUN.OVL in my home directory?

The file IBM$RUN.OVL contains the color palette information for the NetWare menus. Normally, this file is located in the SYS:PUBLIC directory. However, if you ran the COLORPAL utility from your personal directory to change the menu colors, then this file was copied to your home directory automatically. The file is only necessary if you need to use colors other than the menu defaults.

How can I find out which user ID corresponds to my user name?

If you have rights to SYSCON, use it to display your user ID. Follow these steps:

1. Execute SYSCON.

2. Select User Information.

3. Select your user name.

4. Select Other Information.

This displays the user ID for the selected name, as shown on the next page.

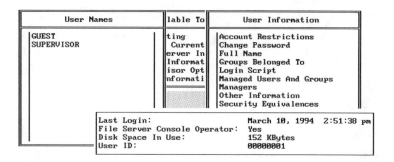

How can I administer rights to a directory from the command line?

Use GRANT to assign rights and REVOKE to take them away. The syntax for GRANT is

GRANT *rightslist...* FOR *path* TO [*user or group*] *name* /*option*

The syntax for REVOKE is

REVOKE *rightslist...* FOR *path* FROM [*user or group*] *name* /*option*

You can replace the variable *rightslist* with any of the standard values discussed in Chapter 2 (read, write, filescan, and so on). The /S option enables subdirectories, and the /F option enables files.

FILER and NDIR seem to be ignoring my MAP ROOT commands. Why?

MAP ROOT was never intended to be a security feature, so the FILER and NDIR utilities can bypass it. Currently there is no workaround, so if security is an issue, remember not to give users access to these files.

Why does FILER invoke the HELP utility when I exit?

You are using an older version of FILER that has been known to exhibit this behavior periodically. You can obtain a newer version of FILER from NetWire.

When I'm running FILER or NETADMIN, what does NetWare mean by the message, "Attempt to open the Unicode table has failed"?

Some of your environmental settings are insufficient. To operate properly, text utilities require both a FILES = 50 and BUFFERS = 20 statement in CONFIG.SYS.

How can I use a batch file to log out?

Log in as a supervisor equivalent and use an editor to create a batch file (for example, BYE.BAT), as follows:

```
MAP F:=SYS:LOGIN
F:
LOGOUTIN
```

Store this file in a directory to which all users are mapped. Create another batch file (for example, LOGOUTIN.BAT), as follows:

```
NLOGOUT
CLS
LOGIN
```

Keep this in the SYS:LOGIN directory. When BYE.BAT is executed, it logs in to F: (SYS:LOGIN) and calls the LOGOUTIN file, which logs the user out, clears the screen, and runs LOGIN. As a result, after logging out, the screen displays a login prompt for the next user.

After upgrading from NetWare 2.15 to 3.11, all of my NetWare utilities display in black and white, yet other applications (such as WordPerfect) come up in color. What's wrong?

Your CMPQ$RUN.OVL file may be corrupt. Rename this file, and then go into COLORPAL. COLORPAL will create a new CMPQ$RUN.OVL, and this should fix the problem. Execute COLORPAL with the public directory as the default directory of the OVL file (wherever the current default is), or the new file may be created in the wrong place.

Acronym List

This appendix provides a listing of the acronyms that appear in this book, as well as many other computer, NetWare, and networking acronyms that are helpful for NetWare users to know.

AC	alternating current
ACDI	Asynchronous Communication Device Interface
ACK	acknowledgement
ACL	Access Control List
ACS	Asynchronous Communication Server
ADSP	AppleTalk Data Stream Protocol
AEP	AppleTalk Echo Protocol
AFP	AppleTalk Filing Protocol
AGS	Asynchronous Gateway Server
ALM	Application Loadable Module
AMI	alternate mark inversion
ANSI	American National Standards Institute
API	application program interface
ARP	Address Resolution Protocol
ARPANET	Advanced Research Projects Agency Network
ASP	AppleTalk Session Protocol
ASPI	Advanced SCSI Programming Interface
ATP	AppleTalk Transaction Protocol
ATPS	AppleTalk Print Services
BC	block check
BIOS	basic input/output system
BPDU	bridge protocol data unit
bps	bits per second
BRI	Basic Rate Interface
CCITT	Consultative Committee for International Telegraphy and Telephony
CLNS	connectionless network services
CMIP	Common Management Information Protocol
CMOT	Common Management Information Protocol Over TCP/IP
CPE	customer premises equipment
CSMA/CD	carrier sense multiple access/collision detection
DARPA	Defense Advanced Research Projects Agency
DCB	disk coprocessor board
DCE	data circuit-terminating equipment
DDP	Datagram Delivery Protocol
DET	directory entry table
DIB	Directory Information Base
DIX	Dec Intel Xerox

DL	data link
DMA	direct memory access
DOD	Department of Defense
DPA	Demand Protocol Architecture
DSAP	destination service access point
DSU/CSU	data service unit/channel service unit
DTE	data terminal equipment
DTR	data terminal ready
DTSX	data transport station for x.25
EBIOS	Extended BIOS
EIA	Electronic Industries Association
EISA	Extended Industry Standard Architecture
ESF	Extended Superframe Format
FAT	file allocation table
FCS	frame check sequence
FDDI	Fiber Distributed Data Interface
FDM	frequency division multiplexing
FLeX/IP	File Transfer Protocol (F), Line Printer Daemon (L), and X Window support (X).
FSU	file support utility
FT-1	fractional T-1
FTP	File Transfer Protocol
GMHS	Global Message Handling Service
GPE	general protection error
GPPE	general protection processor error
HDLC	High-level Data Link Control
Hz	hertz
ICMP	Internet Control Message Protocol
ICP	Internet Control Protocol
IDE	Intergrated drive electronics
IDP	Internetwork Datagram Protocol
IEEE	Institute of Electrical and Electronics Engineers
I/G	individual/group
IOC	inter-office channel
IP	Internet Protocol
IPC	interprocess communication
IPX	internetwork packet exchange
IRQ	interrupt request

ISA	Industry Standard Architecture
ISDN	Integrated Services Digital Network
ISO	International Organization for Standardization
IXC	Interexchange Carrier
K	kilobyte
Kbps	kilobits per second
KHz	kilohertz
LAN	local area network
LAP	Link Access Procedure
LAP-B	Link Access Procedure-Balanced
LAT	Local Area Transport
LATA	Local Access and Transport Area
LEC	local exchange carrier
LED	light-emitting diode
LIP	Large Internet Packet
LLC	Logical Link Control
LSL	Link Support Layer
MAC	Media Access Control
MAN	metropolitan area network
MAU	multistation access unit
MB	megabyte
Mbps	megabits per second
MHS	Message Handling Service (Novell)
MHz	megahertz
MLID	Multiple Link Interface Driver
MMAC	multimedia access center
MSIPX	MicroSoft Internetwork Packet Exchange
MTTR	mean time to repair
NACS	NetWare Asynchronous Communication Services
NAK	negative acknowledgement
NASI	NetWare Asynchronous Services Interface
NBP	Name Binding Protocol
NCP	NetWare Core Protocol
NCSI	Network Communications Services Interface
NDIS	Network Driver Interface Specification
NDS	NetWare Directory Services
NetBEUI	NetBIOS Extended User Interface

NetBIOS	Network Basic Input/Output System
NFS	Network File System
NIC	network interface card
NLM	NetWare Loadable Module
NOS	network operating system
ODI	Open Data-Link Interface
OSI	Open Systems Interconnection
OSPF	open shortest path first
PAD	packet assembler and disassembler
PAP	Printer Access Protocol
PBX	private branch exchange
PDN	public data network
PDU	protocol data unit
PEP	Packet Exchange Protocol
PIC	peripheral interrupt controller
POP	point of presence
PSTN	public switched telephone network
PTS	primary time server
PVC	permanent virtual circuit
QLLC	Qualified Logical Link Control
RAID	redundant arrays of inexpensive disks
RBOC	Regional Bell Operating Company
RFC	request for comments
RI	routing information
RII	routing information indicator
RIP	Routing Information Protocol
RSPX	remote sequenced packet exchange
RTS	reference time server
SAA	Systems Application Architecture
SAP	Service access point
SAP	Service Advertising Protocol
SCSI	Small Computer System Interface
SDLC	Synchronous Data Link Control
SEF	source explicit forwarding
SFT	System Fault Tolerance
SLIP	Serial Line Internet Protocol
SMB	server message block

SMS	Storage Management System
SMTP	Simple Mail Transfer Protocol
SNA	Systems Network Architecture
SNAP	Subnetwork Access Protocol
SNMP	Simple Network Management Protocol
SONET	Synchronous Optical Network
SPS	standby power supply
SPX	sequenced packet exchange
SR	source routing
SRI	Stanford Research Institute
SRT	source routing transparent
SRTS	single reference time server
STP	shielded twisted pair
STS	secondary time server
SVC	switched virtual circuit
TB	transparent bridging
TCP/IP	Transmission Control Protocol/Internet Protocol
TDM	time-division multiplexing
TFTP	Trivial File Transfer Protocol
TIC	Token Ring Interface Coupler
TLI	Transport Layer Interface
TP	twisted pair
TSR	terminate and stay resident
TTS	Transaction Tracking System
UAM	User Authentication Method
UART	universal asynchronous receiver/transmitter
UDP	User Datagram Protocol
U/L	universal/local
UPS	uniterruptable power supply
UTP	unshielded twisted pair
VAN	value added network
VAP	value added process
VIPX	Virtual IPX
VLM	Virtual Loadable Module
VMS	Virtual Memory System
WAN	wide area network
WNIM	wide area network interface module

XMS	Extended Memory Specification
XNS	Xerox Network System
ZIP	Zone Information Protocol

Glossary

Asynchronous transmission   A method of transmission in which each information character is individually synchronized, usually by using start elements and stop elements.

Availability   The percentage of time that a particular function or application is available for users.

Bandwidth   The difference between the limiting frequencies of a continuous frequency band.

Baseband transmission   A method of transmission in which digital signals (1s and 0s) are inserted directly onto the cable as voltage pulses, without modulation. Each signal uses the entire spectrum of the cable. This scheme does not allow frequency-division multiplexing. Ethernet is an example of a baseband system.

Bit   The smallest unit of information a computer can process.

Bridge   An internetworking device that connects two similar local area networks running the same LAN protocols. A bridge operates at the Media Access Control (MAC) layer of the OSI model.

Broadband transmission   A method of transmission in local area networks in which coaxial cable is used to provide data transfer by means of analog (radio frequency) signals. Digital signals are passed through a modem and transmitted over one of the frequency bands of the cable. The original IBM PC network was a broadband system.

Bus A LAN topology in which stations are attached to a shared transmission media. The media is a linear cable; transmissions travel the length of the cable and are received by all stations.

Byte A group of eight bits representing a character of data.

Carrier sense multiple access/collision detection (CSMA/CD) A Media Access Control technique for bus and tree LANs. A station wanting to transmit first senses the media and transmits only if the media is idle. The station ceases transmission if it detects a collision. LocalTalk and 802.3 are examples of CSMA/CD.

Cheapernet A baseband local area network that uses a thinner cable and less expensive components than Ethernet or the original IEEE 802.3 standard. Although the data rate is the same as Ethernet (10 Mbps), Cheapernet has a smaller network span and a smaller allowable maximum number of taps.

Coaxial cable A cable consisting of one conductor, usually a small copper tube or wire, within an insulator and surrounded by another conductor of larger diameter, usually copper tubing or copper braid.

Collision A condition in which two packets are transmitted over a media at the same time, and their interference makes both unintelligible. This condition occurs on CSMA/CD networks.

Cyclic redundancy check (CRC) An error-detecting code which is the remainder resulting from dividing the bits to be checked by a predetermined binary number.

Data compression The process of shortening the length of records or blocks by eliminating gaps, empty fields, redundancies, and unnecessary data.

Data-link layer Layer 2 of the OSI model. This layer converts an unreliable transmission channel into a reliable one.

Differential manchester encoding   A digital signaling technique in which a transition in the middle of each bit time provides clocking. The encoding of a 0 is represented by the presence of a transition at the beginning of the bit period; a 1 is represented by the absence of a transition.

Distributed data processing   A type of data processing in which some or all of the processing, storage, and control functions, in addition to input and output functions, are dispersed among data processing stations.

Dual cable   A type of broadband cable system that uses two separate cables: one for transmission and one for reception.

Electronic mail   Correspondence in the form of messages transmitted between workstations over a network.

Encryption   The process of converting plain text or data into unintelligible form by means of a reversible mathematical computation.

Error-detecting code   A type of code in which each data signal conforms to specific rules of construction, so that departures from that construction in the received signal can be detected automatically.

Error rate   The ratio of the number of data units in error to the total number of data units.

Ethernet   A 10 Mbps baseband local area network specification developed jointly by Xerox, Intel, and Digital Equipment Corporation. It is the forerunner of the IEEE 802.3 CSMA/CD standard.

Facsimile   An image transmission system. The image is scanned at the transmitter, reconstructed at the receiving station, and duplicated on paper.

Federal Communications Commission (FCC)   A regulatory agency that rates computer products for radio transmission interference. For example, a class A rating means the product is good for commercial/office use; a class B rating means it is good for home use.

Fiber Distributed Data Interface (FDDI)   A fiber-optic cable standard for a 100 Mbps optical fiber-ring local area network.

File server   A computer that provides each workstation on a network access to shared files. Access to a file is usually controlled by the file server's software rather than by the operating system of the computer that accesses the file. (NetWare is a file server operating system.)

File transfer facility   A distributed application that transfers files and portions of files between computers.

Full-duplex transmission   A method of transmission in which data travels in both directions at the same time.

Gateway   An internetworking device used to connect two computer networks that use different communications architectures.

Half-duplex transmission   A method of transmission in which data travels in either direction, one direction at a time.

Header   System-defined control information that precedes user data.

IEEE 802   A committee of the Institute of Electrical and Electronics Engineers organized to produce standards for local area networks.

IEEE 802.2   A superset of the other 802.x protocols that allows interconnection.

IEEE 802.3   A successor to Ethernet as the CSMA/CD network architecture.

IEEE 802.4   A token bus network.

IEEE 802.5   A token ring network.

Internet   A collection of communication networks interconnected by bridges, routers, or gateways.

Internet Protocol (IP)   An internetworking protocol that executes in hosts and routers to interconnect a number of packet networks.

Internetworking   Communication among devices across multiple networks.

Layer   In a network architecture, a group of services, functions, and protocols that is complete from a conceptual point of view, is one of a set of hierarchically arranged groups, and extends across all systems that conform to the network architecture.

Local area network (LAN)   A communications network that provides interconnection of a variety of data communicating devices in a small area. A LAN makes use of a shared transmission media and packet broadcasting; a packet transmitted by one station is received by all other stations. Typically, a LAN has either a bus, tree, or ring topology.

Manchester encoding   A digital signaling technique in which there is a transition in the middle of each bit time. 0s are encoded with high levels during the first half of the bit time; 1s are encoded with low levels during the first half of the bit time.

Media Access Control (MAC)   For a local area network, the method of determining which station has access to the transmission media at any time. Common access methods are CSMA/CD, token bus, and token ring.

Microcom Networking Protocol (MNP)   A common error correction protocol for modern data communication.

Modem (modulator/demodulator)   A device that converts digital data to an analog signal for transmission over a telecommunication line and then converts the received analog signal to data.

Multiplexing   In data transmission, a function that permits two or more data sources to share a common transmission media such that each data source has its own channel.

Network interface unit (NIU)   A communications controller that attaches to a local area network. It implements the LAN protocols and provides an interface for device attachment.

Network layer   Layer 3 of the OSI model. This layer is responsible for routing data through a communication network.

Open System Interconnection (OSI) reference model   A model of communications between cooperating devices that defines a seven-layer architecture of communication functions.

Optical fiber   A thin filament of glass or other transparent material through which a signal-encoded light beam is transmitted by means of total internal reflection.

Packet   A group of bits that includes data and control information. This term generally refers to a network layer (OSI layer 3) protocol.

Packet assembler/disassembler (PAD)   A functional unit that enables data terminal equipment not equipped for packet switching to access a packet-switched network.

Packet switching   A method of transmitting messages through a communications network in which long messages are subdivided into short packets. Each packet is passed from source to destination through intermediate nodes. At each node, the entire message is received, stored briefly, and passed to the next node.

Physical layer   Layer 1 of the OSI model. This layer manages the electrical, mechanical, and timing aspects of signal transmission over a media.

Presentation layer   Layer 6 of the OSI model. This layer manages data format and display.

Print server   A program and/or hardware that processes print queues by copying the contents of the print queue to the print device. PSERVER is an example of a print server.

Private branch exchange (PBX)   A telephone exchange on the user's premises that provides a circuit-switching facility for telephones on extension lines within the building, and access to the public telephone network.

Protocol   A set of semantic and syntactic rules that determines the behavior of functional units in achieving communication.

Protocol data unit (PDU)   Information containing control information, address information, or data, that is delivered as a unit between peer entities of a network.

Remodulator   In a split broadband cable system, a digital device at the head end that recovers the digital data from the inbound analog signal, then retransmits the data on the outbound frequency.

Repeater   A device that receives data on one communication link and transmits it, bit by bit, on another link as fast as the data is received, without buffering.

Response time   In a data system, the elapsed time between the end of the transmission of an inquiry message and the beginning of the receipt of a response message, measured at the inquiry terminal.

Ring   A LAN topology in which stations are attached to repeaters connected in a closed loop. Data is transmitted in one direction around the ring and can be read by all attached stations.

Router   An internetworking device that connects two computer networks. It uses an Internet Protocol and assumes that all attached devices on the networks use the same communications architecture and protocols.

Service access point (SAP)   A means of identifying a user of the services of a protocol entity. A protocol entity provides one or more SAPs for use by higher-level entities.

Session layer   Layer 5 of the OSI model. This layer manages a logical connection (session) between two communication processes or applications.

Spectrum   An absolute, contiguous range of frequencies.

Splitter　An analog device for dividing one input into two outputs and combining two outputs into one input. It is used to achieve tree topology on broadband LANs.

Star wiring　A method of laying out the transmission cable installed for a local area network. All cables are concentrated in a wiring closet, with a dedicated cable running from the closet to each device on the network.

Subnetwork　A portion of a network that operates as a complete unit.

Synchronous transmission　A method of transmission in which the occurrence of each signal representing a bit is related to a fixed time frame.

Systems Network Architecture (SNA)　The communications architecture used by IBM. SNA is also implemented on many other vendors' computers to provide connection to the IBM world.

Tap　An analog device that permits signals to be placed on or removed from a transmission media.

Teleconference　A conference between persons at a remote distance from one another linked by a telecommunications system.

Terminal emulation　The capability of a personal computer to operate as if it were another type of terminal linked to a processing unit.

Token bus　A Media Access Control technique for bus and tree LANs. Stations form a logical ring, around which a token is passed. A station receiving the token may transmit data and then must pass the token to the next station in the logical ring.

Token ring　A Media Access Control technique for ring LANs in which a token circulates around the ring. A station may transmit data by seizing the token, inserting a packet onto the ring, and then retransmitting the token.

Topology   The way in which the end points, or stations, attached to a network are interconnected. The common topologies for LANs are bus, tree, and ring.

Transmission media   The physical media that conveys data between data stations.

Transparent bridging   A bridging technique that places the intelligence of the bridging function in the bridge.

Transport layer   Layer 4 of the OSI model. This layer provides reliable, sequenced transfer of data between endpoints.

Tree   A LAN topology in which stations are attached to a shared transmission media. The media is a branching cable emanating from a head end, with no closed circuits. Transmissions propagate from any station to the head end and then throughout the media, and are received by all stations.

Twisted pair   A transmission media that consists of two insulated conductors twisted together to reduce noise.

Underwriters Laboratory (UL)   An organization responsible for regulating powered devices for safety.

Videoconference   A teleconference involving video. The video may be full motion video or some lesser quality scheme.

Virtual circuit   A packet-switching mechanism in which a logical connection (virtual circuit) is established between two stations at the start of transmission. All packets follow the same route, need not carry a complete address, and arrive in sequence.

Voice mail   A computerized system for recording and delivering recorded telephone messages.

Wiring closet   A specially designed closet used for wiring data and voice communication networks. The closet serves as a concentration point for the cabling that interconnects devices, and as a patching facility for adding and deleting devices from the network.

Index

Have we answered all your questions?

If you would like to **speak to the experts** who wrote this book, **call** Corporate Software's Novell® Certified Tech Support. Certified NetWare® Engineers (CNEs) will assist you with Novell 3.x and 4.x installation, Novell Utilities usage, user and upgrade issues and technical problem resolution.

1-800-477-7583 $95 per problem. (Major credit cards accepted)

1-900-555-2005 $3.95 per minute. (First two minutes free)